BEING SUGAR RAY

BEING SUGAR RAY

THE LIFE of SUGAR RAY ROBINSON,
AMERICA'S GREATEST BOXER
and FIRST CELEBRITY ATHLETE

KENNETH SHROPSHIRE

BASIC
CIVITAS
BOOKS

A Member of the Perseus Books Group
New York

Books published by BasicCivitas books are available at
special discounts for bulk purchases in the United States by
corporations, institutions, and other organizations. For more
information, please contact the Special Markets Department at the
Perseus Books Group, 11 Cambridge Center, Cambridge, MA 02142,
or call (617) 252-5298 or (800) 255-1514, or
e-mail special.markets@perseusbooks.com.

Designed by Trish Wilkinson
Set in 12-point Goudy

Library of Congress Cataloging-in-Publication Data

Shropshire, Kenneth L.
    Being Sugar Ray : the life of Sugar Ray Robinson, America's greatest
boxer and first celebrity athlete / Kenneth Shropshire.
        p.   cm.
    ISBN-13: 978-0-465-07803-5 (alk. paper)
    ISBN-10: 0-465-07803-6 (alk. paper)
    1. Robinson, Sugar Ray, 1920- 2. Boxers (Sports)—United
States—Biography. I. Title.
GV1132.R6S57 2007
796.83092—dc22
[B]
                                                    2006032289

10 9 8 7 6 5 4 3 2 1

To my family and friends for their support.
To those who did it right as well as those
who would have, but got stopped short.
Finally, to those who still have the opportunity
to accomplish something special—make it happen.
The moment is over before you know it.

Photo: Corbis.

Boxing is the sport to which other sports aspire.

—George Foreman

CONTENTS

Preface:
Why Sugar Ray?

Concerning athletic stardom, my Stanford football story isn't very grand. As a successful All-City high school center graduating in 1973 from Dorsey High School in Los Angeles, I had earned a college scholarship to the school that had won the Rose Bowl in 1971 and 1972. My celebrity aspirations were high even though at six foot one and 210 pounds I was small for an offensive lineman. The plan when I was recruited was to shift to a defensive position such as linebacker. I started at center on the Gunther Cunningham–coached freshman team, but at the varsity level that "smooth" transition never really happened. On the few occasions when I was allowed to suit up at the next level, I never got in the game—not for a second. At the end of those games, I would head into the locker room in a clean white uniform alongside the grass-stained, bloody stars who had actually played. On those Saturdays, I never intercepted a pass, sacked a quarterback, or did a dance in the end zone. Still, I had a uniform and I was part of the Stanford University team. To the young children who flocked to our home games, the uniform made me almost as much a star as Tony Hill, the starting wide receiver. The kids wanted autographs. In the fleeting moments when these kids asked me for an autograph, I knew (or at least thought I knew) what it was like to be on the other end when someone thinks you are famous. Not surprisingly, some piece of me loved that instant of celebrity attention and adoration and wished there had been more: at least *one* Ray Lewis dance after a big tackle. But in the last analysis, I wasn't at all a celebrity—I was not even ticking a minute off the Warhol fifteen-minute allowance. Still, these experiences were among the first to open my eyes to the powerful narcotic qualities of celebrity—for those on both sides.

Many years later, I would find myself starstruck to a degree that none of those youngsters on any of those Saturdays could possibly have imagined. The scene was the Los Angeles Sports Arena during the 1984 Olympics, and I was the Los Angeles Olympic Organizing Committee executive in charge of Olympic boxing. All in the arena knew my status because I was one of the few wearing a tie in the middle of a typical arid Los Angeles summer. In the midst of the clamoring crowds, I saw him. It was Muhammad Ali, the *greatest*. Without question he is the biggest celebrity athlete of all time. I saw him, and then lost sight of him. I kept hearing a sound in my ear—like sandpaper on a wooden block—but when I looked there was nothing. After a few such false alarms, I saw a massive commotion at a side entrance. With Don King up front, a dozen or so black men casually strolled into the arena past the bemused and awestruck ticket takers. I blinked again and Ali was standing in front of me, hand extended. The smile on his face impishly said, *"Don't mess with me, I'm having a great time."* I'd seen that same smile, and those eyes, when he'd sparred verbally with Howard Cosell. Television doesn't do it justice. He was a *bad man*.

He had me captivated and he knew it, too. He stood not more than a foot away and proceeded to rub his thumb and forefinger together: sandpaper on a wooden block.

With the slightest slur—a preview of the Parkinson's that would prove him mortal—he said, "You didn't know what was goin' on brotha, didya?"

He then struck a boxing pose as fierce and fluid as if it were 1964. I threw my hands up as if to say, "Not me!" Don King cackled at my surrender and yelled, "Let's go!" When I turned, the Champ was gone—along with his entourage. The next time I saw Ali and his colleagues, they had somehow commandeered ringside seats despite the multiple layers of security we had in place.

No surprise. I'll admit, Ali was one of few celebrity athletes who seemed capable of taking anyone under his spell. In meeting Ali and in considering how he had gone from being Cassius, the Louisville Lip, to the greatest, one can't help but think of Sugar Ray Robinson—the man Ali had admittedly emulated early in his own career and whom Ali asked to serve as his manager (Robinson declined). In a discussion of either man, there is an obligation to be clear about the Ali-Sugar Ray connection. No matter how much credit we give (or Ali himself gave) Robinson as a transitional racial celebrity figure, there is no doubt that Ali pushed the issue of racial pride over the hump of public acceptance.

In his wonderful book, *Serenity*, Ralph Wiley—the wittiest and savviest of sports writers—drew his own conclusions with no prompting from me. Ali "was a Robinson who never deferred to whites," he wrote. "Convention at that time meant subservience on the part of black men. Muhammad Ali simply said, 'I am the greatest,' and in so saying spoke volumes. To me at least." Just before Ralph died I prodded him, without success, to compare the two great fighters; he simply said, "It was a different time." Regardless of the nature of the psychic interplay between these two men, the point remains that even Ali, *the greatest of all time*, would not be where he is had it not been for Sugar Ray.

Celebrity, and nothing else, gave Ali's entourage access to one of the toughest tickets at the 1984 Olympics. And can I really blame myself for letting Ali and crew breeze by me? As much as I'd worked with other athletes and celebrities as a Century City attorney before taking the Olympic job, like the rest of us, I'm only human. How deeply wired is this reaction to celebrity? Here's a story that may provide some of the answer.

From inside a small wire cage a tiny, maple-eyed monkey named Wolfgang peers anxiously at a lab-coated technician. Sherry, Dart, and Niko sit nearby, waiting. The young scientist turns a dial and the lights in the windowless lab begin to dim. The café-au-lait monkey, a male rhesus macaque, edges closer to the heavy wires and caresses a button of his own. He knows what's going to happen.

Wolfgang takes a quick slurp of cherry juice—the drink-of-choice for caged lab monkeys everywhere—from the hollow aluminum tube connected to a small dispenser outside the cage. A moment later, a computer generated image appears in front of him. It shows the hindquarters of a female rhesus, a breeder: slim, maybe or maybe not in heat (there is no telltale pheromone scent to give context to the picture), but judging by Wolfgang's reaction she's nothing special as monkeys go. The monkey fingers his control button idly, but doesn't press it. The monkey takes another slurp of cherry juice and waits. He's played this game before.

The first image disappears and a second one flashes on the LCD screen. It shows a male: full face, same species. Again there is no scent, only an image. Field records show he was the highest-ranking male in this monkey's harem. The alpha male.

The computer flashes again and an image of the ordinary female reappears. The young male squawks and madly presses his button. The picture of the *celebrity* monkey returns. He leans over for a lick of treasured cherry juice, but the dispenser has shut off. Normally, this would bring an angry screech and a rattled cage, but the monkey doesn't care. He stares at his "hero" contentedly until the image changes again, via the technician's hand, back to the ordinary female. Once again, the button; once again, no juice. The monkey gets upset whenever his celebrity disappears; he's willing to forego any amount of juice if he can only gaze at his dream image. The cycle repeats, minute after minute, day after day, with a variety of male macaques, until its meaning is statistically clear.

Even a *glimpse* of a celebrity is worth all the cherry juice on earth.

You've probably seen rhesus monkeys before. They're as indispensable to medical and behavioral research as computers and white jackets. The Rh factor in your blood was named after tests involving the rhesus. These primates in the Duke University slide experiment were so anxious to see a "celebrity monkey" that they were willing to pay every drop of their most prized possession, cherry juice, for the privilege.

Like most experiments involving the rhesus, this one has enormous implications for we higher, more evolved, more discerning and sophisticated primates. The lab game forced the monkeys to pay for their pleasure with juice—like spending money to buy a ticket for a rock concert, movie, or sporting event—to view the celebrities we want to see up close and personal. Even monkeys, it seems, are obsessed with the stars.

How much would you spend to gaze upon a dream? The paparazzi know a great photo will bring them plenty of juice. Athletes know it, too. They get big bucks for showing their faces on everything from trading cards to credit card commercials—and the gravy train doesn't stop there. Most celebrities know the value of their likeness: to retailers, to manufacturers, and to Hollywood. But they seldom understand why other people—supposedly rational ticket-buyers and shoppers—do such irrational things just to view their idols or to own a copy of some product they possess. The answer is simple. We all want the *rewards*—money, jewelry, beautiful cars, mates, accolades, adoration—that celebrities enjoy; we want to *be* the object of our glowing admiration. Many of us think that maybe by getting closer to celebrities, by learning all about them—even imitating the way they walk and talk and dress—we'll share a tiny sliver of that magic and ephemeral dream. After all, imitation is more than the sincerest form of flattery: It's how we learn some of life's most important lessons, from tying our shoes to raising a family; from how to lose gracefully to ways of looking and feeling like a winner. Like rhesus monkeys, being starstruck is in our genes.

Professor Paul Gilmcher explains the Duke monkey experiment this way: "People are willing to pay money to look at pictures of high-ranking human primates. When you fork out $3 for a celebrity gossip magazine, you're doing exactly what the monkeys are doing. The difference between [the] study and *People* magazine is that the monkeys actually know the individuals in the picture."

Unlike the celebrity monkeys in Gilmcher's experiments, the human celebrity like Ali is able to use the awe his celebrity inspires for more than juice-related perks. At first it gains small favors—good seats in restaurants (or at Olympic events), better hotel rooms, a doctor who makes house calls at three in the morning. Later, lunch at the White House, keynote speeches at big conventions, and public forgiveness for one's youthful (or even not so youthful) transgressions. It's always been that way with big celebrities, and Ali's understanding of the nuances of fame and the manner in which he cultivated it can be traced directly back to Sugar Ray Robinson. The difference with Sugar Ray was that it seemed to be part of his game plan from the beginning, or at least part of someone's game plan for him.

Sugar Ray will be our primary guide in this trek through the celebrity athlete's universe. His image appeared on the covers of *Time*, *Life*, *Sport*, and *Sports Illustrated* when black faces and the mainstream media didn't mix. While shadow boxing and skipping rope, his infectious smile was beamed into millions of homes on *The Ed Sullivan Show*. He built businesses and friendships—in Harlem and abroad. In his constancy of character and continual self-creation, he did more than master a brutal sport and enchant a nation in the grip of hot and cold wars, and he truly led the way by inventing an entirely new industry: *the modern black global celebrity athlete*.

According to boxing's bible, *The Ring* magazine, Robinson logged 175 victories between 1940 and 1965—110 by knockout—and only nineteen losses with two "no decisions," boxing's version of a tie. In a sport where most hang up their gloves by their mid-thirties, virtually all of Sugar Ray's defeats came after his fortieth birthday.

Before Sugar Ray, a boxer could be "a slugger" or "a dancer" or "a showman," to name a few of the hard-earned epithets sports writers loved to hang on champions. It was the rare boxer who combined even two of those traits. When it came to Robinson—certainly best known for dancing—they simply ran out of superlatives. He did it all. He was dashing, he had a movie-star's charisma, he had hands faster than Houdini's and legs that belonged in the New York City Ballet. He could take a punch as well as deliver a knockout blow while moving backwards. Even boxing's scoreboard ran out of digits. Robinson had already won 126 fights (and lost only one) when he *began* his reign as middleweight champion—and went from there to win the middleweight title five times. By comparison, Muhammad ("I am the greatest!") Ali went 56–5 and Joe (the Brown Bomber) Louis, 68–3—for their entire careers.

Uniquely, at his 1950s peak, Robinson owned thriving businesses on the west side of Seventh Avenue between 123rd and 124th Streets in Harlem. Sugar Ray's Café, Edna Mae's Lingerie Shop, Golden Glovers Barber Shop,

Sugar Ray's Quality Cleaners, and other businesses offices and apartments were all part of the Robinson empire. It was typical to see his custom pink Cadillac parked out in front of any one of them.

Robinson, like all celebrities, was a product both of his own efforts and of his times. Though he was loved by millions, history dealt him a few cards from the bottom of the deck. Sometimes he got caught reaching for that bottom card as well. There were moments when "America's favorite fighter" became America's most notorious military deserter, tax evader, or worse. Sugar Ray was occasionally his own worst enemy. For every person who admired his confidence and success, others stood in the wings just waiting for him to fall.

While he was in his prime, negatives surfaced as his success rose: being difficult to deal with even to the extent of canceling fights, his arrogance in personal relationships—although not projected broadly publicly—his womanizing, and the alleged physical abuse of family members during the prime years of his career. In 1953, the legendary black sports writer Sam Lacy probably captured this dark side best when he wrote in his column, "I have said here many times in the past that, in my opinion, Sugar Ray Robinson was the greatest athlete in a given field I have had the pleasure of observing. . . . I have also said here many times that he can be one of the most disgusting figures one is compelled to meet in his business." The closer you get in

time and space, the less chance there is of finding genuine
perfection in any person.

With that and other bumps taken into account, even his
name has the power of myth. From Sugar Ray Leonard to
Sugar Ray Seales, Sugar Ray Richardson to Sugar Shane
Mosley, many other sports figures (and even a modern
singing group) have looked to the Robinson legacy for
power and permanence. Although they all evoke the patina
of the original, none has successfully matched his overall
brilliance, nor the range of his success.

Although he was a giant of his times, as compared with
Jack Johnson, Joe Louis, and others, Sugar Ray Robinson
was not a big man. He was only five foot eleven, and his
weight hovered between 150 and 160 pounds for most of
his career. But as the perennial basketball all-star Allen
Iverson (Sugar Ray's double in size statistics) proves, size
alone does not put points on the scoreboard, nor records in
the books. Unlike Louis, Johnson, Jack Dempsey, and Rocky
Marciano—human tanks who outweighed Ray by as much
as 50 pounds—Robinson was the size of the average man,
and that physical similarity, regardless of skin color—was
one of the secrets of his tenure as a sports celebrity. Today's
image makers struggle to help fans identify with giants such
as Yao Ming and Shaquille O'Neal, but sports fans of the
1940s and '50s really *believed* they could "be like Sugar Ray."

He was the first fully formed celebrity athlete as we con-
ceive of that phrase today. He was black, and he broadly

celebrated that blackness as a dominant feature of his life. This was not a moderated image in the style of Joe Louis or Jackie Robinson, nor was it a Jack Johnson type of over-blown and intimidating presence. By successfully project-ing that he was every man's "everyman," even though he was black—and complex—Robinson became a celebrity not just for his times but for the ages.

His legacy still surrounds us. It accrues dividends for sports superstars blissfully unaware—and some supremely grateful—that they were and are his heirs: champions such as Muhammad Ali, Joe Montana, Venus Williams, Michael Jordan, Martina Navratilova, Jim Brown, Kobe Bryant, Magic Johnson, Tiger Woods, John McEnroe, Lance Armstrong, Billie Jean King, and Derek Jeter. These are the modern sports superstars who have rede-fined athletic celebrity in the twenty-first century. They are the first generation of sports superstars who under-stand the wisdom—and the power—of *being* Sugar Ray, even if they know little or nothing about the man.

ACKNOWLEDGMENTS

For the traditional facts of Sugar Ray's life, I recommend my friend Herb Boyd's *Pound for Pound* (2004), an invaluable companion to this rumination. Boyd does a great job exploring the immense positives and negatives of a life, particularly the negatives of Ray's womanizing and absentee fathering; there are lessons, certainly, to be drawn from those. For the classic "as told to" autobiography, by all means read *Sugar Ray* (1970), which Robinson coauthored with the *New York Times* columnist Dave Anderson—although it paints an understandably sunnier picture. Boyd and Anderson were kind enough to speak with me at length as I moved forward on this project. These, as well as Gene Schoor's 1952 biography, *Sugar Ray Robinson*, provide good primers for the subject you are about to explore. This is a portrait of an elusive figure whose eyes will follow you around the room. It is the biography of an *idea* as well as the story of one man.

As is true at the completion of any long-term project, there are many people I should thank, and I'm sure that I will miss half of them. First, Sharese Bullock. I have some notes dated 1998 that she prepared for me as an undergraduate research assistant. That may have been the first moment of commitment by me to get this done. Sharese is now a grown woman. That memo followed Farah Jasmine Griffin's suggestion that I pursue the project. Then I mentioned it to Keith Harrison, in a casual conversation. He pointed me to an article on Robinson by David A. Nathan in the *Journal of Sports History*. My good friend and sometime coauthor Todd Boyd jousted with me on a lot of this, as did my writing group/Penn colleagues Tukufu Zuberi, Guy Ramsey, Camille Charles, Barbara Savage, Herman Beavers, and Leslie Callahan.

Research along the way was done by present and former students Scott Brooks (with whom I coauthored a piece), Michael Auerbach, Bridget Lawrence-Gomez, and Melissa Shingles. I thank them all. Thanks also to Susan Rayl for reading an early version of the book proposal. Exceptional research assistance was also provided by a number of librarians at the libraries at the University of Pennsylvania as well as the Library of Congress.

I offer a huge amount of thanks to Jay Wurts who as editor and writing coach played the key role in transitioning me (as far as I've made it) to being a writer read by wider audiences. Thanks also to David Shoemaker for first believing in this at Basic*Civitas* and to Chris Greenberg for picking up the ball upon his departure.

People in and out of the boxing world have given me invaluable help and advice. I particularly thank my one-time client, the former Olympic heavyweight gold medalist Henry Tillman, and his trainer, Mercer Smith, who helped me understand the game. My work at the 1984 Olympics brought me into contact with people patient enough to teach me the basics; and the casual conversations I've had with insiders in recent years in order to polish my boxing chops have been enormously helpful. I thank them all.

Thanks go to others, including the boxing historian Bert Randolph Sugar and Robinson's former business manager, Sid Lockitch, who formally allowed me to interview them. Along with others, they are cited appropriately throughout.

Finally, much here is probably going to strike some negatively. I take all the credit for that.

My now thirteen-year-old daughter, Theresa, spent a good part of her young life watching me read, think, and write about Sugar Ray and celebrity. She would ask, "Daddy, are you still working on *that* book?" My wife, Diane, and my son, Sam, were a bit more patient. One of my colleagues at another institution put it even more succinctly: "You keep talkin' about Sugar Ray, man. You gonna write that damn book or not? Just do it!" A bad paraphrase of a good Nike ad, but just as motivational.

Here it is.

PART ONE

SUPERSTARDOM

Sugar Ray on the shoulders of rivals on the gala evening celebrating his retirement in Madison Square Garden, December 10, 1965. Photo: Corbis.

CHAPTER ONE

ADULATION

"Here he comes! Here *he* comes!"

Twelve thousand white faces turn jubilantly up the aisles toward the Fiftieth Street side of Madison Square Garden. Hundreds of fingers jab the air in the same direction. A lone black figure appears, dramatically back-lit. Years later, Sugar Ray's son, Ray Robinson II, described his father as a "cute chocolate baby." Exactly.

A smattering of applause. A spotlight clicks on from above the darkened Garden. Now the applause falls in steady sheets, like rain on a Manhattan pavement.

It is 9:30 P.M. on December 10, 1965, and the heart of America's boxing community has come to the Garden to say farewell to Sugar Ray Robinson. When at last he steps into that final spotlight, the applause becomes a deluge punctuated by cheers and whistles. The Champ pauses, drenched with adulation. When he finally moves down the aisle, most fans see only his upper torso—his legs are obscured by fans rising to applaud from the cheap seats. Robinson floats down the aisle like that scene that always appears in Spike Lee films.

The physical feature most people first noticed about the Champ was his jet black, processed pompadour hair— perfectly molded by a never-seen-in-public black do-rag made of silk. Robinson was one of a handful of blacks—a few recording artists such as the Temptations and James Brown, who, along with higher-class pimps and a host of high-rolling brothers from Harlem and Harlem-like communities rejected the close-cropped, natural *Quo Vadis* haircut of the day. Like almost everything else that truly mattered about the Champ, his charisma *appeared to be all natural*. His shimmering black face, like Nat King Cole's, amplified his beauty. At forty-four, he undoubtedly added some hair dye—china-black—to the process mix, but only because his legend, and maybe his ego, then in the driver's seat of his life, demanded it. If anything, the man knew how to maintain that public image. At this point in his life, Sugar Ray's job was to look like Sugar Ray—for the fans and for himself.

Halfway down the aisle, Robinson looks up and flashes his patented porcelain-tile, movie-star smile—achieved

without modern cosmetic techniques. Robinson continues on through blue clouds of acrid smoke from the unfil-
tered Chesterfields, the Lucky Strikes, the cheap White
Owls, and the Swisher Sweets, whose tiny flames dotted
the darkened Garden like fireflies in the night sky. Without the smoke, the whole place would stink of spilled
Pabst, Blatz, Gilby's, and Old Crow.

"*Thank you . . .* " Robinson mimes as he nears the
ring. He spreads his arms as if to embrace the crowd. A
mighty roar hugs him back. No one seems to care that it
was not always that way.

The exact attendance that night was 12,146, almost all
of it white: men wearing white shirts, dark jackets, and
ribbon-thin black ties. The few women scattered around
the big hall were girlfriends and boxers' wives. Laila Ali
and Jacqueline Frazier-Lyde were still two generations
into the future; and *Million Dollar Baby* was a film no sane
screenwriter would pitch.

Ray pauses on the ramp and circles—counterclockwise,
like a hurricane—raising one hand, then both. The crowd
roars and he continues ringward. His face reflects the
growing excitement. The cheers and whistles are now
joined by chants and stamping feet. This sort of farewell is
rare for any man or woman in any sport; it is a small notch
below the time Lou Gehrig stood before a cluster of microphones in Yankee Stadium in 1953. And this is for a
black man in 1965.

Given that this retiring fighter had come to put on a show without his gloves, the reaction was extraordinary. Headlining the card that night was a world welterweight championship bout between Emile Griffith and Manny Gonzalez—a title Robinson himself had held almost twenty years before. The fight was set to begin at 10:00 P.M., when millions of viewers would snap on their Philcos and Sylvanias to join the RKO-General network's coverage of what, in those days, was a rare nationally televised championship bout. Sugar Ray's farewell would have been televised then, too, but Robinson—never one to count his chips in front of the dealer—wanted cash up front if his name was going to be used to bring in viewers.

"I'm sorry, but you'll have to pay me," he told executives in response to what they assumed was their generous offer: to let the ex-Champ participate—without compensation—tonight in this major broadcast. Many people shook their heads at Sugar Ray over that one, but the only sense as strong as Ray's sense of pride was that which accurately gauged his self-worth. The red lights on the television cameras stayed dark for the next thirty minutes. The promoters should have known better.

As Robinson dances toward the ring, he looks surprisingly graceful—almost feminine. He wears what the columnist Jimmy Breslin called a "finger-tip" robe—white terry cloth cinched tight at the waist with SUGAR RAY in pink on the back—instead of the long blue-and-white silk robe he

so often wore before a bout. The slitted sleeves of the robe
accentuate Robinson's feline grace. To modern eyes, this
farewell outfit might smack of Frederick's of Hollywood
more than of Everlast. If Sigmund Freud had been Sugar
Ray's wardrobe stylist, he might've chosen a Brooks Brothers suit. But inside the showy robe is a man for all seasons;
and boxing, that most naked of sports, is as much about
the heart and head as it is about muscles.

With the near nakedness and overt masculinity of boxing comes an undercurrent of sexuality that's sublimated
in other sports. This shows up in various ways: from the
sexual abstention practiced by many boxers before a bout
to the flexing and preening that goes on at the weigh-in
ceremony or when entering the ring. Robinson, in and
out of the ring, epitomized the sexual overtones of black
men and boxing—strong stuff now, let alone in the 1940s
and '50s.

Before Robinson, the black heavyweight champion Jack
Johnson tried to play this card, but with a predictably heavy
hand. He trained before crowds with a gauze-wrapped pe-
nis bulging beneath his cotton shorts—not for safety, but
for the crowd to see. He purposely played on the sublimi-
nal fears of white men and the secret fantasies of white
women. This proved to be a destructive tactic; eventually,
it backfired, at least in Johnson's failure to acquire long-
lasting positive fame. Sugar Ray was not blind to this
lesson. His "mind games," unlike Johnson's, were aimed at
beating the opponent but rarely at humbling the crowd.

Although Ray's spirit never failed him during his long career, his body—invincible as it appeared—turned against him in the twilight years. He began to get hurt. Those injuries led directly to that night's farewell. You don't stay a *champ* by taking punches. Throughout his career, Robinson dished out punishment with the best of them, usually better than the other guy, and sometimes with deadly results. One of his victims, Jimmy Doyle, went down for the count and that knockout became a fatality. Death never buys a ticket, but it always has a ringside seat.

Three years before Ray's gala retirement, Emile Griffith killed Benny "Kid" Paret in the same ring. Reporters heard Paret call Griffith a *mariçon*, Spanish slang for "faggot," at the weigh-in—more sexual mind-games—and many assumed that the insult turned a big-league bout into a death match.

Somehow, Sugar Ray turned boxing's traditional sexual charge into something much closer to true *eros*. Though boxing has always been a macho game, prize fighters— who know the risks better than anyone—occasionally hug, and even kiss, at center ring when a grueling bout is over. In the closing years of Mike Tyson's brutal career, the audience watched in astonishment as Tyson tenderly wiped a drop of blood from Lennox Lewis's face after a world championship bout in Memphis.

A few observers of the Tyson-Lewis moment were even reminded of those Magic Johnson-Isiah Thomas mid-court kisses—brotherly pecks on each cheek—before their heated NBA encounters in the 1980s. Violence can be calculated, but in its purest form it's rarely without emotion. The difference between a champ and a chump is often measured by the way that emotion is handled. Sugar Ray was a ringmaster of the circus of feelings that boxing produces. He was not the first boxer-entertainer, just the first whose performances came so completely from the heart and mind.

Back at the Garden, Robinson's silk trunks—white with black stripes—peek out from below his robe. His dancing feet are clad in black boxing boots with white laces. A few attendees grumble that the former middleweight champion is coming to his farewell party as if suited-up for a bout. For them, it's the same offense a middle-aged baseball manager commits by taking the field in a beloved big-league uniform with a beer-gut hanging over his belt. But baseball managers don't play, and Robinson—still in great shape, despite his injuries—needs nobody's permission to behave as if he owned the ring. Some fans think he should be wearing a tuxedo; the Sugar Ray *they* prefer is a showman and a class act. Most of the crowd, however, seems to agree with Ray. As the man who has most fully embodied the *spirit* of the game, he should appear only in "uniform"— in the trunks he has so often worn to glory. His hands aren't taped, there are no gloves (you don't load a gun unless you intend to shoot). In this way, the letter of the sport is preserved as well as the spirit, even for the purists. The Champ isn't there to hurt anyone tonight, nor is he there to take more licks from the press.

Missing along with the red-lit television cameras on that night was the commercialism we know today. Sugar Ray wasn't there to endorse any product but himself; he was there because his affection for the sport and his fans demanded it. The printed program had no pictures of Ray wearing Nikes, or Adidas, or Reeboks. No banners floated over the arena, no ads showed Ray touting the virtues of the latest sports drink. That part of the celebrity game was in its infancy and there were few opportunities for black athletes, champions or not, to cash in on their hard-won fame. Razor, beer, and cigarette ads featuring white sports stars in various guises weren't uncommon in the main-stream media; but black athletes, like black Americans in general, just didn't show up on Madison Avenue's radar. Even one of America's favorite pop singers, Nat King Cole, had an otherwise stellar variety show cancelled because of the lack of a national sponsor. In his day, Cole was as successful at vocalizing as Frank Sinatra, but the value of his name on anything but a record label wasn't even considered.

So much had changed in America since the zenith of his career. Race relations in America had taken on a new dimension. Less than a month earlier, during one long, hot week in August, black men had thrown Molotov cocktails at storefronts and rocks at passing motorists in the Watts Riot. The whites in the Garden that night had watched those angry black faces for five days and nights on television before buying tickets to honor one of "*them.*" Superficially, Sugar Ray resembled many of the thousand black men who'd been wounded, or the thirty-five who died, or the tens of thousands who had raged, bled, and fought for a "title" of a different kind. As Robinson was being feted by this mostly white crowd, the embers of that awful week still smoldered.

But Sugar Ray was no ordinary black man, nor was he a black man aspiring to be white, an allegation faced by many black celebrities. He was *the Sugar, the Champ*. The men in the audience had put aside their personal prejudices and ignored the searing images of the recent days and weeks. It didn't matter that those who had read the *Saturday Evening Post* and *Sports Illustrated* knew that Robinson's personal finances were a mess; that the seven companies he owned—including Knockout Productions, Inc., and Sugar Ray's Entertainment Corp—were in trouble; that once-flourishing properties were now lost or entangled in the courts. Ray's belief in himself was not easily swayed by such things, either. In the back of his mind— hidden by the glare of all those lights, the flashing cameras, and that fabulous smile—he was still *the Champ*.

Famous men and women are different from most, and famous black men and women more so. They often receive a pass on the racial prejudgments that condemn so many others. "Oh, Sugar Ray Robinson, Nat King Cole, I don't even think of them as black!" The alchemy that works this transformation—that lifts the fans and the object of their affection out of the here-and-now and into the world of legend—is the raw power—the *eros*—of adulation.

As Sugar Ray approaches the ring, the entourage that once shadowed him everywhere is nowhere to be seen—Robinson hasn't been able to punch their meal tickets since the early 1960s. Now it is 1965, and Ray has lost the clout he once enjoyed. As he floats down the last third of the aisle, the SRO crowd comes to its feet. When he reaches the ring, he wisely steps through the *second* of its four maroon ropes. Robinson has no problem making this look graceful. He has done it often enough at the Garden, taking the higher ropes, including before his first fight. He was nineteen then, and on his way to pummel his stablemate Louis "Spider" Valentine for the 1939 Golden Gloves title. Robinson was a pixie-ish teenager, hair unspoiled by chemicals, coiffed in what used to be called a "front," like Floyd Patterson's. His first four-round "prelim" was fought in this ring, too, on October 4, 1940, on the Henry Armstrong-Fritzie Zivic undercard. He took those opponents as easily as, this night, he takes the second rope.

Four former middleweight champions follow him into the ring. First behind him is Carl "Bobo" Olson. He's about the same age, but pasty, overweight; and he's wearing a J. C. Penney's bathrobe that reaches to his ankles. After Bobo comes Gene Fullmer, natty in a blue silk robe, his name written in white script on the back. He, too, wears the middle-age paunch that Robinson has so carefully avoided. Third is Carmen Basilio, ears huge and cauliflowered. His old white silk robe, like the man who wears it, is clearly past its prime.

The final boxer to enter the ring is Randy Turpin: the "British Negro" (as the newspapers called him), who defeated Robinson for the middleweight crown on July 10, 1951, after the Champ had spent more time partying than training during a highly touted tour of Europe. Robinson took back the title a short time later in New York City. Turpin's nappy hair is parted nearly dead center. His tattered robe could be the same white terry cloth he wore when he fought against Robinson fourteen years before. He is the only boxer who looks as fit as Robinson, but he chooses to enter safely above the first rope.

Later, not long after Sugar Ray's farewell and shortly before committing suicide, Turpin will ask Robinson, "What's worse—being a has-been or a never-was?" He believes that Robinson's decision over him is a fraud, that the fight was stopped while Turpin was still "clearing the fog" out of his head after being decked by a Robinson punch. Eight seconds remained in the round. Apparently, the gap between a future "has-been" and a self-proclaimed "never-was" is exceedingly thin, and, sometimes, impossible to bear.

Now, at center ring in the Garden, exactly on cue, the boxers—the almost-weres, the shoulda-beens, and the one-timers—all converge on Robinson. It is here that Basilio jokes to his comrades, "I'll give you a hundred bucks if you drop him!"

Noticeably missing is Robinson's most famous nemesis, Jake La Motta. In 1947, La Motta had thrown a fight in Madison Square Garden and admitted it to a congressional committee a few years before Robinson's farewell. The fans might've forgiven him, but not the New York State Boxing Commission. He was the only major ex-champ in Sugar Ray's portfolio to be barred from the ring at the big event.

Two old fighters on each side, Robinson is hoisted into the air. He waves one hand and holds on with the other. He gives the crowd his patented, imperial "aw shucks" grin and the audience goes wild.

After five minutes, the gallant litter bearers put Robinson down in center ring. Judge Vincent Impellitteri, the former mayor of New York, appears next to him. He gives Robinson a gold trophy that sits on a tall wooden base. On its crown is a little statue of a boxer, arms raised in victory. The inscription reads, "The Greatest Boxer Who Ever Lived." One of New York's leading black papers, the

Amsterdam News, had promised a week before that Vice President Hubert Humphrey would present the trophy. They are wrong. For reasons more related to the shifting sands of Southern politics and the civil rights movement than the honor of "the greatest boxer who ever lived," the white champion of black civil rights is a no show.

Ray puts the trophy down and the crowd goes silent. "This is the first time I've ever had an experience like this," the Champ says with his usual humility. Normally he would conclude that remark with something like, "What can I say but thank you!" and leave the stage without further comment; but tonight is different.

"I don't know at this opportune time to be happy or sad. I thank God for this and all the other blessings I've received. I'd like to pay my thanks to the boxing commission and all the fellows in boxing who helped me, and most certainly the press who've done a wonderful job in keeping the sport alive." Robinson's voice cracks: "This is not goodbye, but it is farewell to a career that has spanned a quarter century. I'm not going to say goodbye. As they say in France, it's *a tout a l'heure*—I'll see you later." On cue, the singer Gordon MacRae begins and "Auld Lang Syne" fills the arena.

When the festivities at center ring end, Robinson changes in Garden dressing room number 30, a place where he had so often put on and taken off another sort of "game face."

Ten minutes later, he is dressed in an immaculately tailored one-button blue suit, starched white shirt, and black tie. He motors downtown to a celebratory midnight supper at Mama Leone's restaurant with his third wife, Millie—a dignified, soulful woman with little of her husband's panache but all of his heart—by his side. His first manager always liked to end a big evening with a steak dinner, and Ray had taken to some of the finer points of living. Like the quick study he was, the Champ had grabbed that metaphorical steak with both hands and added more than a little sizzle of his own. His trademark pink Cadillac was one example, as were the pink Lincoln Continental and series of blue Buicks preceding it.

By the time of his farewell party, all the cars are long gone. Tonight, Ray pulls up before Mama Leone's in a nondescript American-made station wagon and gets out as the flashbulbs pop and a whoop goes up from the hastily gathered crowd. Ray's famous smile, along with the flashbulbs, add even more sparkle to a glittery Times Square night. It's the mid-1960s, so the flashy welcome is more than expected by the fans, photographers, and celebrities in attendance; and it is appreciated, too.

In those days, all publicity was good if your name was spelled correctly. Superstars did not yet encounter the aggressive paparazzi we know today, photographers who'd sell off their firstborn for a picture of a celebrity caught off his guard. The public then wanted to cherish their heroes, not ambush them. If celebrities needed a bit of time to prepare themselves, put on their makeup, a hairpiece, or the "game face" the public expected, the newsmen happily gave it to them. When Robinson entered Mama Leone's that evening, it was the Ray Robinson fans expected. Along with the stiff drinks and blood-rare steaks, he was the prime entrée on the bill of fare, and nobody forgot it.

The big party is held upstairs. Getting there means running a gauntlet of well-wishers, some bearing trophies and certificates, and at least a hundred more hoping for handshakes and photos. Sugar Ray gallantly plays his part. John Lindsay, New York's mayor-elect, takes advantage of the opportunity and presents Robinson with an award on behalf of the city. He accepts it graciously and the newspapers snap their picture. Others elbow closer to shake his hand. One is still a relative newcomer to professional boxing: Cassius Clay, now known—and derided, in some circles—by the adopted name of Muhammad Ali. The former light heavyweight champion Jose Torres waits patiently behind him. A sports writer beats them both.

"Hey, ol' buddy!" Robinson pumps the man's hand enthusiastically. He has no idea who it is until his wife tells him later at dinner. That's how Robinson greeted reporters and others whose names he could not remember. The last thing he wanted to do was make anyone feel

small or embarrassed—even those he met in the ring.
Every city in America had at least one sports reporter
who just *knew* he was Sugar Ray's pal.

And so the night wears on. As the crowd begins to
thin, the lights come up. The tables are quietly cleared.
Millie leans over to Ray and whispers, "I think we're supposed to leave." Ray doesn't want to go. He doesn't want
to *let* go. But Millie is more than a wife. Not everyone ap-
preciates her, especially Ray's "first" family, and rightly so.
But she is the gatekeeper and she is now the spirit of their
life together. She has slept next to greatness and has seen
when it causes pain, and when it is in pain. She has felt
that pain herself. She knows when to make the call.

As Ray shakes hands with the short-jacketed waiters,
Millie guides him gently but firmly toward the stairs,
then out the door. They make their way to the parking
lot. The attendant has their station wagon waiting, en-
gine running, doors open, ready to go. And so like any
other wistful, retiring man-of-means and memories, the
sports legend drives into the night.

It takes twenty minutes to cross Forty-sixth Street and
drive uptown to his apartment at Seventy-eighth Street
and Riverside. Ray and Millie climb the stairs. He dis-
likes elevators, so he lives in a walk up. That "dislike," we
now know, was really an irrational fear—a terror of small
places gained on his first trip, as a kid, to the top of the
Empire State building—not something a champ likes to

admit, and one reason, perhaps, he craved a view from the top while being very careful about how he got there.

He puts the key in the front door, lets Millie walk in first, then follows. He places his big trophy reverentially on the hardwood floor next to the only piece of furniture in the apartment other than their bed: a beige, vinyl-covered metal card table.

They undress and prepare for bed. This is a bed similar to ones Ray used to lounge on when conducting interviews with reporters after a victory—the bed from which he talked to reporters after the pain of his last fights, the fights where the injuries began to pile up and it took him longer and longer to recover for the next bout. Tonight, though, it is just Ray and Millie—no telephones, no press. The applause has faded. The lights go out. The career is over. He lies there in the dark, staring at the ceiling. It's as if his life had returned to its humble Detroit origins. Then, it was just Ray and his family trying to "make it" way up north. How can he help but mull over, just before sleep, the one question retiring celebrities fear most, and that he himself had been asked earlier that night by a reporter:

"Any regrets over your career?"

He'd simply smiled at the reporter and said, "I'd do it all over again—the same identical way."

On another occasion, Robinson had said, "I went through four million dollars but I have no regrets. If I had a chance to do it over again, I'd do it the same way. I didn't gamble away my money. I used it to let people live. I took my family and my friends on trips with me. I loaned it to strangers to pay their bills, and sometimes I didn't get it back."

CHAPTER TWO

BEGINNINGS

"I'm going to be a champion. You just wait and see."

That's how Walker Smith Jr. introduced himself to childhood friends in Detroit, and later in New York City. He was named after his father, but even then nobody called him by his given name. Everyone called him Junior or Smitty. "Here!" was what Smitty answered when teachers and coaches called "Walker" on the roll, but that was about the only time he heard it.

When Sugar Ray was born on May 3, 1921 (that is the most consistent birth date cited), the Smith family already had two girls. The existence of Ray's older sisters is an indisputable fact. But many of the details of his early life are speculative. We can't be sure when or where he was born. To some extent that is the way Robinson chose to live his life. Spinning a yarn, holding back on details, telling the story the audience wanted to hear—that was part of his genesis legend. It is also possible that he simply did not know.

In his autobiography (ghostwritten by Dave Anderson), he says that he traveled to Detroit from Ailey, Georgia, in his mother's womb. That certainly makes for a more compelling account about where his life began. In fact, many traditional explanations have him born in Detroit. *The Ring* magazine lists his date of birth as 1920. Robinson's birth certificate says that he was born in Ailey in 1921. His sisters were born in Dublin, Georgia: Marie in 1917, Evelyn in 1919.

The Smiths moved to Detroit after receiving a letter from Robinson's Aunt Lillie, who had moved to Detroit a few years earlier with her husband, Herman Hayes. "They wrote back about how easy it was to get a job and how good the salaries were," Robinson stated in his autobiography, "Pop didn't have to be coaxed. He was making maybe ten dollars a week raising cotton, corn and peanuts—mostly cotton." Walker Sr. went first, got a job in the same factory as Herman, then sent for the rest of the family once money was right and he had rented a wood-framed house on Macomb Street. Smith had hopes of that come-and-get-it job on the Ford or General Motors assembly line, but there is no evidence that it ever happened.

In 1927, Sugar Ray's mother took him and his sisters back to Georgia, apparently to escape an abusive husband. Ray pointed to money, and noted that his father had "a few drinks now and then." Once, he heard his mother say to his father, "Don't you talk to *me* about money when you drink up more money than I spend!"

Sprouting up despite the discord between his parents, Smitty was a Roaring Twenties, Depression-era kid; he dressed in wide baggy pants or knickers, many of them patched by Mama, who was a seamstress, and a short-sleeved shirt—usually white—with button-down collars. He often wore a belt cinched correctly at belly-button level. Even with a child's limited resources, Ray knew about style, and he applied what he learned.

The Smith family moved—absent the father and after a year in Georgia—back to Detroit in 1928. That same year, Robinson joined the Brewster Recreation Center, and this is where he was first exposed to boxing. The cost of membership was twenty-five cents per month. It turned out to be the best bargain in American sports.

In Detroit, seven-year-old Junior walked a circuitous route between his home at 222 Macomb Street and the Brewster Recreation Center, between St. Antoine and Hastings. In time, legend has it, he was allowed to carry the tattered gym bag of Joe Louis Barrow, a boxer seven years his senior and already star of the gym.

"I'm going to be the champ one day," he told Barrow.

Joe acknowledged with a backward glance and said, "Yeah, sure," and shook his head at the skinny kid tagging along behind him. Robinson was tall for his age, but light—he was one of the last kids his age to break the gym's eighty-pound barrier. Barrow, on the other hand, had muscle mass to spare, even as a teenager. Later, he would drop the name Barrow.

Brewster Recreation Center sat in what was then known as the Black Bottom section of Detroit—a place long gone except in memory. Robinson wrote in his biography that his part of town was "*Black* because we lived there, and *Bottom* because that's where we are at." Few Detroit natives today know that part of town ever existed, and those who do would be hard-pressed to find its outline on a map.

Robinson dreamed of being champ, but most black men of the day were simply striving to make life better—if not for themselves, then for their children. In 1920s America, there were few clearly defined routes to success for anyone other than Ivy League graduates, Meharry or Howard University–educated doctors or lawyers; or those who owned a family funeral home, barbershop, or beauty parlor business. For blacks, success often meant making the monthly rent, eating at least one good meal a day, and keeping the family together. The nation was segregated, of course—even in the north—and black citizens went second class whether it was to school, to court, to market, or into sports. Robinson's neighbors were often newly arrived black sharecroppers from such exotic places as

Biloxi, Mississippi, and Selma, Alabama: They were just weeks off the farm and only a generation removed from slavery.

Violent racism was still a persistent force of nature. Almost daily, black men were lynched—not just hanged from a tree or a lamp post, but beaten, tortured, and mutilated after death—though most lynchings weren't reported. Calling white policemen to report a white-on-black crime just didn't make much sense. Under these conditions, it didn't take much progress for black people to feel better, and as long as that progress was slow—*real slow*—many white folks didn't object.

Boxing was one of the few venues for black success. When a black man accomplished anything, it gave other black people hope, especially young boys. In a way, boxing was the NBA of its day. Like modern basketball, it gave young blacks the vision of a better life, one filled with money and fame and luxuries; but it was an unrealistic dream for most because a Jack Johnson or a Joe Louis does not come along often. It is a *blessing*, not a right, to earn fame and fortune playing the game you love, as true then as it is today.

Yet even if the ratio of aspirants to champs got better overnight, few mothers in that era, or any other, wanted their sons to grow up to be boxers. Certainly Ray's mother wanted him to have no part of such a brutal activity. When he was young, she was adamant that Ray learn to dance as part of his recreation. And he did. Much of the showmanship he displayed in the ring and out came as a result of those dancing lessons. He learned how to carry himself, how to present himself, how to turn something ordinary, even ugly, into a ballet to remember. It was this foundation that he carried into his post-boxing career, and it put the flair into his future arrival in Paris and his final farewell to boxing in Madison Square Garden. Professional boxing had always been an exhibition, but Sugar Ray turned it into an art.

After moving with her children to New York, Ray's mother, Leila Smith, sought out Dr. Vincent Nardiello of the state boxing commission, a man who would provide ongoing care and counseling to Robinson. Leila asked the doctor whether a fifteen-year-old could handle the rigorous training required of a competitive boxer while he was going to school full time. Nardiello, a practical man, understood the need for any aspiring athlete, no matter what his color, to credential himself for a "day job" while he pursued his dream. He suggested that "Smitty" box part time and put most of his energies into finishing high school—just what Mama wanted to hear.

But from that first day he wandered into the gym at the Brewster Recreation Center, the ring was to be his primary classroom. Gymnasiums in those days were far from the glamour spas we see today; there were no buffed-up trainers, expensive machines, and well-thought-out programs for virtually every sport and age group. More typically, gyms were semi-seedy "men's clubs": pool rooms without the pool tables. Brewster's gym catered a bit more to youth, offering ping pong tables, a swimming pool, and the kinds of "organized" sports commonly played in city parks and vacant lots. But all Ray could see was the boxing ring. It was a world of sweat and blood, liniment and spit; of faded boxing posters and wooden stools; of inverted barrels serving as card tables and first-aid stations; of dusty electric fans that gave little relief from the heat. Ironically, most boxing gyms today still pride themselves as the last bastion of *real* workouts, places where old-fashioned medicine balls and gray sweat suits reign and there's not an ounce of spandex to be found. That was Robinson's new world and he immediately fell in love with it.

Even though Robinson was not allowed by those working the gym to put on the gloves, he was not too young to shadowbox and to take some of the other training, and he began to develop many of the moves that would later become his trademark. "One day Mom noticed me coming up the block, bobbing and weaving and dancing and throwing punches, and she told me later, 'I thought my boy had something wrong with his head, I really did.'"

When he was old enough, Ray undertook the same regimen as his cohorts. He'd do sit-ups on top of a marred wooden table lightly padded with red vinyl. After a few months, the vinyl at end of the table would split—like

the shoddy tuck-and-roll on the booths at a cheap diner—
and begin to cut his shoulders. When this happened, Ray
would get down, turn the table, and keep going until the
other end split, at which time some veteran club fighter
would nag the manager or custodian into repairing the
tear with tape; and so the exercise went on, at least until
the tape ran out.

After a workout, in another corner of the gym, Ray lies
on a different table wearing nothing but cotton shorts
and a towel. A gym masseur, always a big guy and often
a pleasantly punch-drunk ex-fighter, applies liniment
to Ray's aching muscles, rumbling, "This will give you
life, boy . . . it takes a good massage to bring you back
around." This elixir of life is nothing more than alcohol
mixed with ammonia and witch hazel, but for Robinson
it is the sweet smell of success. After a while, a boxer
with talent got "handlers," an odd collection of trainers,
would-be managers, and scruffy gofers who stand around
and kibbitz during this process. Occasionally, one of
them might drop a buffalo-head nickel into a rusty coffee
can that never strays far from the masseur's field of vision.
A sign above it reads MASSAGE 5 CENTS.

  With nothing to do on the table, Ray scans the other
hand-scrawled signs on the gymnasium wall, though
they are by now familiar to even the greenest boxer: NO
SMOKING, NO SPITTING ON THE FLOOR, YOU

MUST THROW YOUR TAPE AWAY. There's nothing about NO HITTING BELOW THE BELT or NO RABBIT PUNCHES, but that's the kind of stuff you learn in the ring.

An assortment of well-worn training equipment crowds the dingy space. Some is leather, tan or black; some canvas, orange or red; but all of it is for boxing. There are speed bags (those oblong basketball-like hanging targets that good boxers can play like a Buddy Miles drum), heavy bags (big duffles filled with sawdust or even BBs), and protective gear for head, hands, and groin. Ray might not have felt like a champion when he first got in the ring, but weighed down with all that armor, he knew he was a gladiator.

He uses one of the gym's two full-sized rings. At the corner of each, on the floor, just down from the platform, is a metal bucket. At the end of a three-minute sparring round, Ray and his partner retire to opposite corners, lean across the ropes, and spit blood and saliva into the buckets. After a session of a half-dozen rounds, half an inch or so of a dirty, translucent pink phlegm swirls at the bottom. Hard to believe, but Robinson would say later that he came to need such training in the same way that an addict needs dope.

Although the color of the fluid in the spit bucket is a constant reminder that blood is always the essence of a blood sport, bleeding of any kind is a boxer's natural enemy. Under pummeling by heavy gloves, a small abrasion can become a cut, a cut a tear, a tear a rip that shows tissue down to the bone. Trainers do what they can to prevent it: from mouthpieces to guard teeth to Vaseline smeared around the eyes, eyebrows, and nose. They also administer a lot of training outside the ring: less bloody, but just as demanding. One of the most important exercises for a fighter is shadowboxing: feinting and jabbing the air. Ray keeps his feet a shoulder-width apart, keeping his balance, making sure his weight doesn't shift too far in any direction. An off-balanced fighter is an out-of-control fighter, and when you lose control you lose fights.

He is also taught to focus on arm position. "Keep that arm tucked in!" the trainers shout, but he flops his elbow like a chicken wing, more intent on landing a punch than protecting himself from a blow. Such reckless aggressiveness may make a kid feel like a champ, but it's the fastest way to get your back applied to the canvas. To keep that errant right arm locked down for defense, yet coiled enough to deliver a knockout blow, they give Ray a rolled-up newspaper to stick under his arm. Ray saw this drill from the earliest days in Detroit: If the copy of the *Detroit News* didn't fall as the boxer sparred, then he'd got it right. Before long, Ray learns the first rule amongst fighters: You can't win if you're knocked out. He hears the mantra a hundred times: "Protect yourself at all times."

But staying safe doesn't win a fight. You've also got to hurt your opponent. A generation after Robinson's initial training, one of his namesakes, Sugar Ray Leonard, was having a problem with swollen hands. This may sound minor—after all, a boxer's well-taped hands are encased in padded gloves—but a boxer's hands are his primary weapons, offensively and defensively. Some old timers think they should be protected even more than the boxer's head. The legendary trainer Angelo Dundee solved Leonard's problem by taping his hands with Kotex tampons, which buffered the pain of parries and punches. This trick was known to many in Robinson's gym, and it's one of the reasons some of our best young fighters are the product of our oldest trainers.

Cornermen are the handlers who look after the gladiator while he's in the arena, and the best work with the skill and precision of a surgeon. They store tape in what looks like an old fishing tackle box, but they can tear and twist those inch-wide rolls like origami. When a session is over, the masterpiece of wrapping is simply cut off with surgical scissors: tempered steel blades curved to a 135-degree angle to allow speed and accuracy—and no bloodshed.

Young Walker already knew the workings of a gym like the back of his glove, but it was only after he and his then-fatherless family moved to New York that his boxing life truly began. Robinson described his first street fight in his autobiography. It happened when he was about thirteen years old. "I started flailing," he said, "no jabbing or dancing, just swinging. Somehow I popped him on the nose and his blood was all over him and me and the sidewalk. He dropped his head to look at the blood, and I hit him some more and knocked him down. I jumped on top of him and punched him some more."

Ray's "success" in this artless first fight surprised him. It was just a dispute between kids. The two had been racing between sewers with friends when a push became a shove and the shove was followed by punches. Robinson didn't want to lose face in front of his friends; he knew that if he didn't strike back, he'd be labeled the neighborhood pushover.

At the gym, armed with his street-corner confidence, he found believers in his boxing prowess who would help him move forward in the fight game. Knowledgeable trainers and handlers began to see that his talent was something special. By the time he was eleven—a skinny kid at Cooper Junior High School in 1932—he entered the ring for his first organized fight: a three-round Police Athletic League (PAL) contest. Ray won this first decision. Shortly afterward, Benny Booksinger, director of the local PAL, took Robinson to the Salem Crescent Athletic Club, where he was introduced to the man who would become his long-time trainer: George Gainford, who coached the gym's boxing team.

Gainford was one of the most successful boxing trainers in Harlem. He was a bear of a man: He was more than
six feet tall and weighed two hundred and fifty pounds.
His brown skin was the color of grizzly fur, though his
manner was anything but beastly. Gainford was a generation out from the West Indies, and he could command a
clipped British accent when it was needed to make his
point. Under Gainford, Walker Smith Jr. left the world of
boxing and Sugar Ray Robinson entered it. How the
name change came about reveals something of both men.

Soon after joining Gainford, Walker Smith Jr. was on a
boxing road trip with his trainer and other boxers. Much
like Amateur Athletic Union youth basketball teams of
today, teams of boxers would travel from city to city to box
other teams; usually, one boxer represented each weight
category. There was an opportunity for Smith to have a
bout, but he lacked the appropriate credential. Gainford
was resourceful. Another of his protégés, a kid named Ray
Robinson, had a license but had dropped out of the program, returning the card to Gainford. Which are you more
attached to, Gainford essentially asked young Smitty, your
boxing or your name? His next fight, in the flyweight division, saw a younger, lighter, but new and improved "Ray
Robinson" enter the ring. It was an easy enough name to
remember, and one the world would never forget.

But like many new athletes, Ray and others in Gainford's stable often got nervous before a fight. At Starbuck

Arena in Watertown, New York, in 1939, Gainford was determined to get Robinson and the others to relax.

"What's that?" a young boxer asked as Gainford set up an old Victrola on one of the tables in the locker room.

Some of the older fighters and those from families who had a few dollars knew a record player when they saw it and laughed lightly, though they knew Gainford was all business before a fight and the machine wasn't there for a party.

Gainford put on a record—jazz, up-tempo with a sizzling beat—and asked the young boxers, "What do you think of that?" Faces lifted, nervous toes began to tap. A young guy, newly named Robinson, got up and started dancing. His teammates began to clap. He went on that evening to win his bout.

This pre-bout Victrola ritual and Robinson's later victory prompted the sports editor of the Watertown *Daily Times* to tell Gainford, "That's a sweet boy you have there."

"Sweet as sugar!" George replied.

The name stuck. The next day, the *Daily Times* praised the performance of a new fighter called "Sugar Ray Robinson."

In 1939, Robinson began collecting Golden Gloves victories—a tournament for amateurs begun in 1923 by the *Chicago Tribune* sports editor Arch Ward, who had the great idea of creating a manly after-school activity (sometimes instead-of-school) for young men who would otherwise have gone looking for trouble. As Ray's standing in his weight division increased, his fame spread beyond the rowdy, seedy, earnest little world of neighborhood boxing to the national press.

As with many of Robinson's big fights, the 1939 Golden Gloves final was held at Madison Square Garden in New York City. Boxing, and particularly Golden Gloves competition, was at the heart of prewar America, and although this fight featured two black kids, earlier rounds included Irish and Italian, Jewish and German kids. Few Latino fighters existed in those days. As it unfolded, boxing aficionados got a foretaste of many such contests to come.

Ray Robinson and Louis Valentine enter the ring looking like twins out to settle a family feud. Many in the crowd know the two are close friends, members of the same Salem Crescent Boxing Club. Their resemblance in size, complexion, body type, and hair style is striking. As the bout progresses, it's clear that they are amateurs. They fuss with their belts, pull up their trunks the way the Big Boys do. When they clash, they flail at each other like angry brothers, not boxers.

Amateur bouts are typically scheduled to last only three rounds. Nine minutes doesn't seem like much, but for beginners, the constant movement, the mental demands of focusing on your opponent, and the strength required to hold up gloves weighing between six and twelve ounces each all take their toll. The first round ends when the referee calls "Break" and the bell sounds. Both boxers retreat to their stools for instruction and a one-minute breather. Because George Gainford is training both at Crescent, he stays away from both corners. Harry Wiley tends Robinson. The one-minute break between rounds hardly seems enough. They take water and listen to their coaches, but neither seems anxious to resume the fight. After the first break, the bell for the next round clangs and they stagger out to center ring.

In this 1939 Golden Gloves bout, the twig-thin Robinson wears white trunks with black stripes and what appears to be an extra-high waistband. It's the only way many in the crowd can tell him from the similarly thin Valentine in black trunks with a white stripe. Overhead, the red, white, and blue bunting that decorates the rafters of Madison Square Garden hangs limp in the heat.

The untutored combat commences as the second round begins: skinny arms and legs flailing, impetuous advances and hasty retreats. But something about this round soon looks different. One of the fighters, the kid in the white trunks, begins to tuck his right arm in like a pro. The left arm jabs and probes for weakness. He keeps his balance. He's on his toes. The more knowledgeable fans and reporters and judges sit up. Something's going on here. It just might be boxing.

The referee, in a new black-collared shirt with GOLDEN GLOVES boldly inscribed on the back, breaks up a clench. Referees in amateur matches often train young boxers as well, and their job, even in tournaments, is to keep the kids "out of trouble." To ring insiders, this means preventing serious injury, nipping bad habits in the bud, and keeping emotions under control. He follows the kids around the ring, straining to keep up as the boxer in the white trunks begins to score some points.

Robinson's blows, though still crude, show a crispness that was lacking earlier. He hits left, right, left, right—solidly but with no master plan, no real power, no subtlety. A commentator would have a tough time calling the hooks and crosses and uppercuts, but a few blows are landing and Valentine seems to be getting the worst of it.

Toward the end of the round, fans catch a glimmer of what will become the Robinson trademark: a left jab setting up a blow with the right, including one or two punches that start with an almost cartoon-like wind up—an early bolo punch. Then he drifts back into his amateurish habits and the two exchange weak broadsides like wounded gunboats.

Toward the end of the second round, Valentine seems to realize he is overmatched. Still, Robinson is wading in too often, arms flailing like windmills, but at least he's looking for openings. Valentine grabs Robinson around the waist. It's not the type of clinch the professional's use but a streetfighter's wrestling hold. The referee moves in for the break, but Robinson has already spun away like a dancer. Valentine closes again on Ray's waist. This time Ray catches him with a solid right and "Spider" Valentine drops like a shot duck. The referee is over him instantly, starting the count.

Valentine is more surprised than hurt. He begins to get up, but slowly.

"*One,*" the Garden hears the referee's voice for the first time. His right finger snaps out over Valentine. He raises the right arm and lowers it again.

"*Two!*"

Robinson is dancing in a neutral corner. His eyes sparkle confidently.

"*Three!*" Valentine is up on one knee.

"*Four!*"

Valentine is on his feet. "*Five!*" The referee wipes off Spider's gloves and points him back toward center ring. Ray marches out to meet him, but the bell soon ends the second round.

After some water and encouragement from Wiley, the bell clangs for the final round. Both fighters look tired. The childlike flailing stops and both men now seem to be taking the fight seriously. They circle on their toes, exchanging jabs. A few combinations get through, but none is a fight-stopper.

The referee stays vigilant for the slightest bit of blood—a common cause for stopping an amateur bout since no headgear is worn in this era—but, despite the occasional flurry of workmanlike punches, no real damage is done.

The final bell. The boxers touch gloves and retire to their corners. The wait for the decision is short.

Robinson has won.

This was a proud first step in the fulfillment of a child-hood dream. Sugar Ray Robinson was indeed a champion of sorts: the winner in the 126-pound featherweight division of an increasingly prestigious amateur tournament that he later went on to win: the national Golden Gloves title. It was Ray Robinson's biggest victory and an important milestone in an undefeated boxing streak that would last until February 5, 1943, and that first loss to Jake La Motta after ten grueling rounds in Detroit.

The next year, 1940, the bunting over the same ring was joined by a glowing GEM RAZOR ad shining brightly above the rafters. Robinson's skills had outdistanced those of his amateur opponents even further—his confidence now reflected in the faces of both fighter and trainer.

When the bell for his bout with the white boxer Andy Nonella sounds, Robinson is shadowboxing in his corner. Gainford, this time properly at his station, throws a towel over his shoulder and nonchalantly steps from the ring. He doesn't look back. Although Ray is moving quickly toward his opponent, Gainford is obviously confident that Robinson will carry out their plan: a blend of boxing basics and a studied refinement of some of the rapid combinations and brilliant footwork Ray had demonstrated since winning that first Golden Gloves title in 1939.

Nonella comes out charging and pushes Robinson down to one knee. Out of more than five thousand boxers who began the competition, Nonella is one of sixteen in the finals of eight competitive brackets. Surviving that kind of attrition is reason enough for any young athlete to be proud and aggressive, so Robinson is understandably cautious. The referee understands this and lets Robinson rise from one knee without the mandatory eight count required when an amateur is knocked down. It was a push, not a punch, and Ray is unharmed. Most of the 17,037 fans know that the fall isn't a big deal for Robinson. On the other hand, it doesn't help when the other guy freely, and literally, starts the bout by pushing you around.

That fall, however, seems to galvanize Robinson. He comes after Nonella with combinations no amateur, however clever in the Golden Gloves, can avoid or deflect. Robinson's speed is striking; it makes the white boxer's responses appear to be in slow motion. But Ray is still a developing fighter. He doesn't know all the tricks, and it shows. Still, commentators are amazed at the difference the past year has made. Robinson connects with a left hook. Nonella, stunned, staggers back. The fight seems to be over.

As the first round nears its end, Robinson hands Nonella a flurry of combinations that sends him into the ropes, then to the canvas near his corner. That initial push and drop to the knee is forgotten.

Robinson closes the bout with a long left hook that sends Nonella reeling. A series of combinations follow without much response. Nonella has now retreated across the ring. Robinson finishes him with a powerful right. This sends Nonella's head and shoulders through the second and third ropes like a steer hung up on barbed wire.

The referee jumps between them and starts what will turn out to be a nine count. The fight is stopped. Robinson is declared the winner in less than sixty seconds.

As the *New York Times* reported, "Referee Bernie Newman stepped between the fighters when it was apparent Nonella had no chance and halted the fray." The Nonella corner ran into the ring and removed their man's mouthpiece.

Robinson had just nabbed another Golden Gloves title and repeated again at the national level. His name was now on the tip of every boxing journalist's pen. No longer carrying the gym bag of an idol, Sugar Ray was on his way to becoming a celebrity athlete in his own right.

In 1940, no one really took notice when a young man dove headlong into such a violent and adult profession. Even today, a boxer's turning professional at an early age is not much of an issue, and it never really was. Boxers have traditionally come from the "dregs of society." From Irish and Jewish immigrants to Negroes, and now Latinos from Mexico, Guatemala, and below, there have been no overwhelming concerns for these individuals.

Still, the occasional "ban boxing" movements have always erupted after a death in the ring. But rarely do we give a thought to young kids who enter boxing at the expense of going to school. Dozens of boxers have entered the ring over the years with the moniker "kid": Kid Paret and Kid Gavilan are two kids on a long list.

Today, most young athletes who dream of becoming professional set their sights on the National Basketball Association, not boxing. Many of these kids are the same ones who, a generation earlier and a foot shorter, made their way to the Brewster Recreation Center in their respective communities and sacrificed life and limb in pursuit of a dream that, ultimately, turned out to be a nightmare.

When little Walker Jr. first showed an interest in boxing, the Smith family had no way of knowing whether he had what it took to make it where so many would fail. The Smith family had no way of knowing that Walker Jr. would shatter so many barriers. Virtually on his own back, he would carry athletes, particularly black athletes, beyond the difficult years of racial segregation into a future of unlimited promise. He would play a pivotal role for the greatest black generation—that was certain from an early date—but he also created a new model for *all* athletes. Like a Solon or Pericles or Augustus, he established a Golden Age for those who would follow: the modern celebrity athlete.

Before Sugar Ray, Joe Louis was always *handled* by those around him. He might have been notorious for his prowess in the ring, but outside those ropes he was under control. He was given specific guidance on how to be loved by white fans and, maybe more specifically, how to avoid being hated by them. Before Louis, Jack Johnson had failed to garner popular appeal. Like any tragic hero, his own shortcomings proved to be his most powerful nemesis. Jackie Robinson was enmeshed in following the rules of Branch Rickey. He made the famous three-year promise to "turn the other cheek," to avoid confrontations on and off the field so that fans, white and black, would admire his courage. Sugar Ray Robinson, on the other hand, saw his opportunities and took them.

Ray's path contrasted most sharply with that of Jack Johnson. Johnson was the first black heavyweight champion (although Tom Molineaux was referred to as the "Champion of America" in 1809). This was no accident of nature, nor was it a tribute to Johnson's skill as a fighter— it was simply that blacks were not allowed to compete against white champions.

In spite of his pioneering victories, the Smith and Hurst families of Dublin, Georgia—Ray's immediate ancestors— probably knew little about Jack Johnson's career and couldn't have guessed how negatively the country would respond to it. These families were, as was much of black America at this time, living in a segregated world where the important news of the day was confined to the price of corn, peanuts, or cotton. Day-to-day living was far more important to them than the emergence of a black superstar or the tearing down of a race barrier. In fact, following sports in the first decade of the twentieth century was a gentleman's occupation; almost everyone else was too busy scratching out a living, especially in rural America.

But where blacks did hear of the news, there was universal elation, at least until leaders such as Booker T. Washington began to wax negatively about Johnson's actions outside the ring: "Jack Johnson has harmed rather than helped the race. I wish to say emphatically that his actions do not meet my approval and I'm sure they do not meet with the approval of the colored race." Heavyweight champ or not, Johnson had single-handedly upset the delicate balance of power and nonpower that white and black America had worked out. He had ripped at the scabs of Reconstruction.

Other black athletes—such as the jockey Isaac Murphy, the first rider to win three Kentucky Derbies, and the bicyclist Major Taylor, had great success before Jack Johnson's triumph. Taylor had global success. In horse racing, fourteen of the fifteen jockeys in the first Kentucky Derby were black. But Johnson was heavyweight boxing champion, and in America this violent blood sport mattered most. Headlines were assured for anything involving the heavyweight division, especially when the sporting events in question flipped the script of the violence between races.

At Johnson's moment, athletics were not constrained by the same racial barriers as were other sectors of society. Boxing authorities blinked and Johnson managed to sneak in to get his shot. This was a "gray" period in America's racial history: Jim Crow rules were spawning their own backlash, but justice would be a long time coming. The leaders of baseball adopted the first formal "whites only" rules at the turn of the century. Blacks, until then, still played regularly in the precursors to the National Football League. Before the institution of the black exclusionary rule in baseball, a number of blacks played professionally at the highest levels—including the bare-handed catcher Moses Fleetwood Walker. It was a brief and shining moment when the sport meant as much as the sportsman; but that was soon to change.

Jack Johnson was the last of these pre–Jim Crow athletes. The happy timing of his birth, coupled with his undeniable raw talent and a winner's will, allowed him to become a champion. It was an "error" that the boxing powers-that-be would not allow to happen again. Once Johnson lost the title, a black man wasn't given the chance to fight for it again until June 22, 1937, when Joe Louis defeated James Braddock, the boxer whose gritty comeback was documented in the film *Cinderella Man*. Of the great black boxers of the day—Sam Langford, Sam McVey, Joe Jeanette—none was given the opportunity to fight for the coveted title. Boxers and promoters just flat out discriminated.

While he held the title for seven years beginning in 1908, Johnson lived large. He drove fancy cars, wore expensive clothes, and was seen with beautiful women, usually white. Years later, Johnson's flashy imagery was natural fodder for Hollywood films such as *The Great White Hope* as well as a Broadway play, *Big Time Buck White* featuring none other than Muhammad Ali in the title role.

America in the early 1900s was not ready for a black heavyweight champion, particularly not this one. Race riots and other confrontations occurred in cities across the country, including Philadelphia, New Orleans, Omaha, and Houston. These erupted after the former title holder, Jim Jeffries—America's "Great White Hope" (as Jack London called him in 1910)—faltered in the Reno, Nevada, championship bout. Jeffries' loss led to a banning of fight film distribution across the country.

The ban was mandated by federal legislation. The image of a black man pummeling a white man, particularly for the heavyweight championship of the world, proved too inflammatory to be shown in America's theatres. The institutionally approved message of the day was *Birth of a Nation*, not birth of a black heavyweight champion. Curiously, this ban marked the high point of federal intervention in the sport, which, both before and after Johnson, tended to be treated with a laissez-faire indifference. The government never took up the cause of those advocating for safer conditions or age limits; rather, they stepped in only when the established racial dichotomy was threatened.

Shortly after Johnson's reign, the world was at war. Blacks stepped up to fight for America, and France was the prime destination for "colored troops" in World War I. This was the beginning of a more modest migration than the one that would bring the Smith family northwards: the relocation of many African-Americans to Paris from 1917 onward. France, in long decline as an imperial power had mostly interacted with blacks from African colonies— there had been no mass exportation of slaves to Europe. Thus Paris was seen as a place where segregation was non-existent, where blacks could live without the consciousness of color. Black Americans experienced a euphoric equality that was all but impossible in the United States. Knowledge of the sanctuary spread throughout black America after the war.

Half a world away, the fatherless Smith family moved to Hell's Kitchen on the West Side—419 West Fifty-third Street—and later to Harlem to gain another kind of opportunity. Friends and relatives told Leila that there was a big demand for seamstresses in New York. The Great Depression was in full swing, and people moved at the mere *rumor* of jobs and wages.

Sugar Ray Robinson would emerge from this stew of desperate dreams and harsh realities to become a key figure in this greatest black generation. From an athletic standpoint, Robinson's early boxing years could not have been more successful. As an amateur, he won eighty-five fights, including those Golden Gloves victories. That number of bouts represents an entire career for many of today's pro boxers. Forget about an apprenticeship, forget about honing your skills and learning your craft as an amateur; today it's all about turning pro and cashing big checks as soon as possible.

The path to professional boxing was often paved by the Olympics. Robinson was not an Olympian, but others—Floyd Patterson, Muhammad Ali, Joe Frazier, Sugar Ray Leonard, and others with strong marquis names—were. For them, that victory stand, itself the product of a lifetime's labor, was a springboard to greater fame. Many of today's young boxers want it all, and they want it now.

When to turn pro has always been a tricky question, especially if an athlete is young. Like any major decision, choosing one path means foregoing others. Turning pro as a very young man made sense for Sugar Ray because there were fewer options for black men then, and little scrutiny once the choice was made. Today, young newly minted pro athletes are given a veritable third degree by fans and the media. This scrutiny is still partially based on race, but other factors also come more prominently into play, including economics, gender, and the standards established by a particular sport. Basketball has increasingly led the way in defining the accoutrements of sports stardom for young men.

LeBron James, who has adjusted well and succeeded on the NBA hardwoods, was criticized by many for making the decision to go straight to the pros from high school. The same for Kobe Bryant, Kevin Garnett, and all the others who have gone on to NBA success straight from high school. Michelle Wie, the teenaged golf phenomenon, is the latest nonblack youngster to turn pro, and she did so with tremendous fanfare. From an economic standpoint, the decision was a no-brainer. While minor league baseball and hockey players toil away in anonymity for a few thousand dollars a month, sometimes a few hundred dollars, the average deal for an entry-level NBA contract, runs to multiple millions.

In golf, Tiger Woods—the first black golfing superstar—"gave up" a Stanford education to join the PGA tour. As a self-proclaimed multicultural "cablinasian," his options were well known. Here was a kid who turned down alternatives other talented people, of any race, would die for. One reason he was able to pass on the Stanford education (as trivial as that looks given his success) had to do with having strong, supportive parents; he had the familial infrastructure, emotional and financial, that was not available to a Depression-era boy like Robinson. Woods truly did have options, but Robinson had to take what was virtually the lone available route.

Easing Tiger's marketing transition and mitigating his risks was his choice to represent himself as an "everyman," not every black man, but *every* man, a task of enormous proportions. He genuinely embraced all aspects of his background—Caucasian, black, and Asian—and showed that, under the skin, we, too, were Tiger. All of this meant that Tiger, unlike some black kid from the 'hood breaking into the NBA, was also closer to *us*, no matter who *us* happened to be.

Undoubtedly his acceptance into the mainstream consciousness was helped by the fact that he excelled at a genteel sport. Unlike a pugilist, you didn't have to be intimidated when Tiger performed. Furthering his accessibility was the physically diverse makeup of the PGA: To shoot par at the local links, you don't have to be born tall, talented, and black, nor do you have to be schmoozed by coaches from a Big Ten university. People identify with Tiger the way they did with Robinson as a nonheavyweight. The rare moments in which the average fans can see themselves reflected in their heroes can be inspiring; it is these fleeting moments that connect so many so deeply to the pastimes that they cherish.

On the other hand, over-identification with our sports heroes can have a detrimental affect on young people. Not every high school senior (or, as is true of Michelle Wie and a few others even younger than that) can compete against seasoned professionals. Too often, "counselors," including athletes who have already achieved success, encourage kids to think that they can *be* LeBron James, Kobe Bryant, or Kevin Garnett. The sobering truth for most youngsters seriously considering a pro career is that they're probably not going to make it.

Still, Robinson is one of the few who overcame the odds time and time again. Even without an Olympic platform, Robinson built his reputation in the boxing world. He did it the old-fashioned way: one fight at a time. The 1940 Olympics were originally scheduled for Tokyo, but with World War II booming, they were moved to Helsinki. When Finland was invaded, the Olympics were put on hold until 1948, and by then Robinson's pro career was well underway. The stories of his early fights were delivered most often in newspaper and magazine articles. Radio broadcasts eventually covered his fights, and later, weekly televised bouts showed an enormous national audience what they'd been missing.

Financially, George Gainford carried Robinson as far as he could. Boxing is an expensive business, and with the demand for constant training, it is difficult for young boxers to hold a job outside the ring. Further complicating the financial aspect of the sport is that boxing managers have earned a reputation for corruption: They have easy access to the fighter's money, and few people look over their shoulders. Typically, a manager keeps one third of a boxer's purse, another third going to various and sundry expenses associated with the fight and its venue. This doesn't leave much for the fighter, whose expenses only increase as he rises in stature and faces tougher opponents. Of course, not all purses are big, and trainer/managers, like venture capitalists, wind up backing a lot of losers before they find a winner. Eventually, it became clear that Gainford simply lacked the financial wherewithal to take Robinson to the top.

Fortunately for Ray, Curt Horrmann, a former star athlete at Cornell and the owner of a brewing company, stepped in to fill this gap. Horrmann had the resources to care for Robinson and Leila Smith as well as the connections needed to get those crucial "next fights" that were the stepping stones for contenders. Not every fighter is so lucky. The wrong manager can sabotage a career not just through fraud or corruption but through ineptitude or the kind of personality that spoils rather than cultivates essential relationships with boxing officials, promoters, and even the press.

It was under Horrmann's leadership and through his connections that the Robinson legend began to develop. Horrmann had the foresight to hire the *New York Daily Mirror* boxing writer Murray Lewin to get Robinson's name "out there." Even Ray's first pro fight—against Joe Echevarria—made the undercard of a world title bout at Madison Square Garden. Robinson was already good when Horrmann found him, but now he was being groomed for greatness.

With this world-class managerial support, Robinson turned pro. His debut against Joe Echevarria on October 4, 1940, ended in a second round knockout. Both the crowd and his paycheck of $150 were sparse, but a great juggernaut had been launched. Over the course of these early fights, Robinson matured quickly. He became known as a slugger, winning five of his first six bouts by a knockout. In his next two years of boxing, most of his fights failed to go the distance. He put his luckless opponents away fast and hard.

As is true today, the lighter weight categories rarely got the same attention as the heavies. Nothing seems to resonate with fans as much as "Heavyweight Champion of the World!" In spite of the public predilection toward heavyweights, the press began paying attention to Robinson, and Robinson didn't let them down. He made "good copy." Gossip columnists such as Walter Winchell and Ed Sullivan liked Horrmann and used him as one of their sources. It was a true symbiosis: Everybody got what he wanted. Everybody won.

Robinson continued to crank out an impressive series of wins before stepping away from boxing for a stint in the military. In 1942, this was not unusual. World War II was in its darkest hours, and Jack Dempsey, Joe Louis, and Gene Tunney had already joined the service. Ray was inducted into the army on March 1, 1943. The cover of the September 1943 issue of *The Ring* magazine showed a uniformed "Private Robinson" taking his country's oath. Inside, photos showed Robinson's good relations with the men at camp, where he taught boxing and led them in calisthenics. Initially he was stationed at Fort Dix, New

Jersey, and later with the Air Corps at Mitchell Field on Long Island. When not giving informal boxing demonstrations for the troops, he guarded airplane hangars. Eventually, Robinson was reassigned to Casual Detachment Z, otherwise known as the Joe Louis Troupe.

When he received his draft notice, Ray had been preparing for a rematch with Jake La Motta, scheduled for eleven days after Ray's February 5 defeat. Knowing the value of sporting events as morale boosters on the home front, the government gave Ray a furlough and the fight went ahead in Detroit on February 26, 1943. Like most American heroes, Robinson began showing up in photographs in military uniform. Although many athletes entered the armed forces in both World War II and Korea, it was still somewhat rare to see a superstar in uniform, but it was not virtually unthinkable, as it is today.

Americans loved seeing their favorite athletes bravely defending the country, and people liked Robinson—at least what they knew about him—although they did not know quite what to make of him. Robinson had yet to be given a shot at a title, in part because he would not participate in the fixes that were sometimes necessary to get the right matches. He was also a boxer that opponents sought to avoid. Robinson said that the dominant boxing promoter of the day, Mike Jacobs, specifically told him that he'd kill the division: "He said, 'I got to have two or three guys fightin' for the title. You'd *darken* the class.'" It was early actions and comments such as this that began to mold Robinson's negativity toward those who controlled boxing.

Race was also a reason for the delay Robinson was facing in getting a title bout. The fear of darkening the division was genuine. The writer W. C. Heinz may have said it best: "In this country, from the turn of the century on, boxing gave the black man, because it needed him, a better break than he received in any other sport, but it only gave him what it had to." Yet his success had been widely trumpeted and people regularly referred to him as the "uncrowned champ" or the "people's champ," just as Muhammad Ali would be praised in later years.

All the while, a boxer by the name of Freddie "Red" Cochrane, who entered the navy, held the welterweight title when Ray entered the army. Even though Robinson would not be fighting him soon, it was natural for people to compare the boxers. Fans also couldn't help but compare Robinson to those who had come before him. From such comparisons one thing became clear: Ray Robinson was no Jack Johnson, neither in physical stature nor in degree of animosity inspired.

The lessons from Johnson's antagonistic relationship with America were not lost on Sugar Ray. He also took note of the ways in which Joe Louis, a much more acceptable form of powerful black man, could succeed him in

1937. To gain public acceptance, and therefore a shot at the title, Louis had become the antithesis of Johnson. Where Johnson had been combative, egotistical, and aggressive, Louis came across as nonthreatening, passive, and deferential, especially when dealing with whites. In the ring, Louis never celebrated a victory over a white opponent. When speaking to the media, he was quiet, even gentle, convincing white fight fans that he was not, as Sonny Liston was labeled a generation later, "that big nigger waiting for you in the alley."

Joe was a quiet champion who controlled his emotions inside and outside the ring. Like Johnson, he had an impact on Sugar Ray, but the lessons they taught were quite different. Robinson saw the value of a flamboyant, audacious personality, like Johnson's, but without the hostile, provocative edge. Joe Louis, on the other hand, led a social life so quiet that it belonged with the obituaries rather than on the front page. The press liked a good story, and Ray decided that his aspirations for continued celebrity required that he provide it. Although never as radical as Jack Johnson, Ray Robinson found his own way to resist racial inequality and oppression: He became the personification of cool. His ability to be outgoing, ethnic, and individualistic all at the same time was something new on the celebrity scene, and the public, black and white, adored him for it. His indomitable boxing talent got him the stage, but it was Sugar Ray's impeccable image that won the applause.

During the war years, however, Louis and Robinson became a team. Their mission was to entertain the troops—under the Brown Bomber's banner—and Ray, with one eye always on the future, had no problem with that. More than twenty years later, Muhammad Ali would shock the world by refusing to enter the armed forces, even after receiving assurances that his principle duty would be to give boxing exhibitions. Times were different; it was a different war. When Ali said, "I ain't got no quarrel with the Viet Cong," he found legions of supporters. Conversely, Sugar Ray and Joe Louis understood completely why America was fighting the Axis, and when they didn't understand, they trusted enough not to ask questions.

For seven months, Sugar Ray toured the United States with Louis and other boxers entertaining soldiers about to go off to war. These exhibitions were so popular that the top brass scheduled them to take their act overseas. They were sent to Fort Hamilton in Brooklyn, where they prepared to ship out. It was the day before their departure when Robinson's rising star fell back to earth.

the foot of the bed, the pa-
W. Smith, had fallen down
ilton. Robinson did not even
er when they came to visit.
Robinson initially talked
hospital disinfectant. He in-
d him—and this from a man
years in a Harlem gym mari-
t. Gradually, Robinson's ver-
fall: a tumble down a blur of
rracks. Now he had a head-
he had ever felt in the ring.

blunt trauma amnesia," was
ved from the parade of white-
s who came and went from his
nd prodded him; they shoved
and shined tiny flashlights in
his heart. They measured his
od and urine samples.

Ray asked after receiving his

doctor said with confidence.
s one, but it should blow over

mnesia, Ray learned, was that
ve it without knowing much
Robinson recovered, he re-

PART TWO

EXPECTATIONS

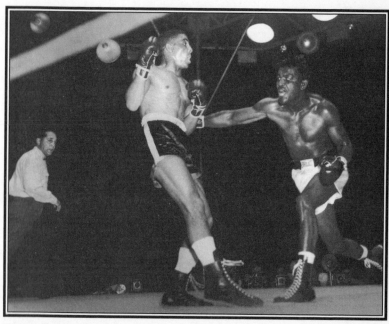

Sugar Ray battling Randy Turpin in a rematch for the middleweight title in New York City September 12, 1951. Photo: Hulton Archive/Getty Images.

According to the chart
tient, an army sergeant na
a flight of stairs at Fort Ha
recognize his wife and mar

After he was revived,
about was the stench of t
sisted that it just about k
who had spent his format
nated in sweat and linim
sion has it, he recalled t
wooden steps outside his
ache, worse than anythir

"You've had an attack
the first explanation he re
uniformed doctors and nu
room. They probed, poke
thermometers in his mou
his eyes. They listened
blood pressure and took

"So what do we do no
diagnosis.

"We wait, Sugar," th
"There's no medicine for
pretty quickly."

The funny thing abou
you can understand you
about anything else. W

should be suspended. Here is the rare occasion when it was the responsibility of the self-aware superstar to cede the spotlight rather than to gravitate toward it.

America's sports celebrities are too often consumed by the very people who love them most—destroyed emotionally and financially, as if sacrificed inadvertently to the demands of fame. But Sugar Ray Robinson was one athlete, and one of the first, who seemed to understand the complicated aspects of our celebrity culture. He knew people expected him to be a star both in and out of his sport, a realization that still escapes many athletes today. This is certainly why the antipatriotism comments stung so severely. Too often, admirable behavior on the field of play turns negative at home, in night clubs, and during interviews. In his heart of hearts, Sugar Ray knew that *he* was no hero beyond what he did in the ring. He also knew that his insight was not shared by the public. To most, he was *supposed* to be something special.

Usually, the press didn't dig deeply when a whiff of shame or scandal was in the air. The Parker story was an exception. Until then, newspapers had a stake in keeping a positive image going. After all, people loved sports stars and wanted to read about them. Today sensationalism, "warts and all" journalism, sells better than hagiography, so virtually anything is fair game. How many "regular folk" could withstand the scrutiny our sports stars regularly receive?

As the flaws of our athletic heroes have become more well-known over the years, the culture at large has learned

Where Ali espoused his ideological opposition to the war in Vietnam and sought draft deferment on religious grounds, Tillman volunteered along with his brother to serve in the army. He wanted to go to Fort Benning, Georgia, and become an Army Ranger. As Tillman explained: "[Football] just seems so unimportant compared to [the September 11 attacks on the World Trade Center]. My great-grandfather was at Pearl Harbor, and a lot of my family have fought in wars. I haven't really done a thing as far as laying myself on the line like that."

Post-Tillman, post–9/11, the modifying word *sports* before "hero" risks becoming a cliché. "Let's hope, *now* that sports are in perspective, we *keep* them there," wrote *Sports Illustrated*'s Rick Reilly a week after the 9/11 attacks. How wonderfully appropriate, then, is Bill Russell's no-autograph policy. Russell was notorious for disappointing fans looking for autographs. Few were satisfied when he would repeatedly say, "I don't give autographs." Fans walked away grumbling. Russell did not explain to them the true message he was trying to convey: Playing basketball is not my entire life and most assuredly not the most important piece.

For every athlete who has been swallowed up by ego there are a dozen full of the same humane impulses as those who pay to see them play. When the NFL was determined to go forward with the games after September 11, they were rebuffed by the head of the players' union, Gene Upshaw, who said that his constituents felt the games

PART TWO

EXPECTATIONS

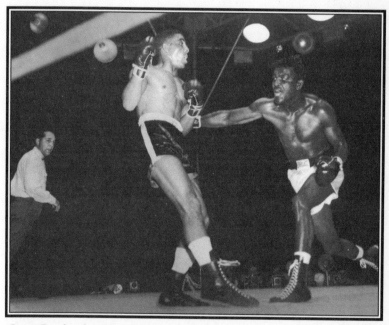

Sugar Ray battling Randy Turpin in a rematch for the middleweight title in New York City September 12, 1951. Photo: Hulton Archive/Getty Images.

CHAPTER THREE

HEROES

On Friday, April 5, 1944, a lithe, muscular black man lay in a too-small, railed bed at the one-thousand-bed Halloran General Hospital on Staten Island. He was dressed in the usual green backless hospital gown. His heavily pomaded hair left an oily residue on the crisply laundered pillowcase.

"That's Sugar Ray Robinson!" a nurse whispered. Attendants paused in their routine to take a look. He had been there a week, and still a few staffers hadn't gotten the word about the star in their midst. Not that there was much to look at even for those who did know. When awake, he was groggy, and he spent most of his time on his left side holding onto his bed for dear life, seemingly consumed by dizziness and nausea.

According to the chart at the foot of the bed, the patient, an army sergeant named W. Smith, had fallen down a flight of stairs at Fort Hamilton. Robinson did not even recognize his wife and manager when they came to visit.

After he was revived, all Robinson initially talked about was the stench of the hospital disinfectant. He insisted that it just about killed him—and this from a man who had spent his formative years in a Harlem gym marinated in sweat and liniment. Gradually, Robinson's version has it, he recalled the fall: a tumble down a blur of wooden steps outside his barracks. Now he had a headache, worse than anything he had ever felt in the ring.

"You've had an attack of blunt trauma amnesia," was the first explanation he received from the parade of white-uniformed doctors and nurses who came and went from his room. They probed, poked, and prodded him; they shoved thermometers in his mouth and shined tiny flashlights in his eyes. They listened to his heart. They measured his blood pressure and took blood and urine samples.

"So what do we do now?" Ray asked after receiving his diagnosis.

"We wait, Sugar," the doctor said with confidence. "There's no medicine for this one, but it should blow over pretty quickly."

The funny thing about amnesia, Ray learned, was that you can understand you have it without knowing much about anything else. When Robinson recovered, he remembered the accident and the names and faces of his friends and family. He was then promptly arrested by the military police. He claimed to be as confused as his fans. He was in such hot water because he had not been on board the ship that was supposed to carry him and the Louis troupe from Pier 90 to Europe. Throughout his life, Robinson maintained that he had no idea why he had missed the ship. But his untimely discharge and the dose of bad publicity that followed were apparently the result of his misadventure.

In trying to get at the truth, W. C. Heinz questioned Robinson years later: Was it amnesia and the hospital or was it desertion? Even after Heinz pointed out that "it was . . . in the record that he [Robinson] had previously declared his intention not to go [with the Joe Louis Troupe to Europe], and that the Articles of War as they applied to the punishment for desertion had been explained to him," Ray was adamant: "But why would a man say such a thing?" he said. Heinz observes that he was asked to ghostwrite Ray's autobiography, but he chose not to do so because Ray refused to resolve this and other "conflicting versions" of events that occurred in his life.

"You may be a good fighter, but you don't fight too good for your country," one fan told Robinson days after his discharge. The insult cut Ray deeply. He may have been back on his feet—even cleared by the docs to start boxing—but the rehabilitation of his image proved to be a much longer haul. The combination of his boxing prowess and the careful manner in which he carried himself outside the ring had caused the public to hold him to higher standards, just as is true of athletes today. His previously sterling reputation was that of a focused fighter, a good guy, and a tough competitor. He was viewed by many as an enviable athlete, and with his induction into the armed services in 1943 he was on his way to becoming a bona fide American hero.

Robinson remembers the "you don't fight so good" insult as coming from a little man in a brown suit whom he had met only in passing. The catalyst for the insult was most likely an unflattering column, written by Dan Parker in the *New York Daily Mirror*, that focused on the alleged desertion. "Robinson is in a bit of a pickle," the columnist wrote. "Leaving the ship which was to carry him overseas with a group of other boxers to entertain the fighting men on foreign fronts, Ray was picked up by the military police after the ship had sailed and now awaits court-marshal." That was on April 7, 1944. But on June 3, 1944, three days before D-Day, Robinson received an honorable discharge. In spite of the "honorable" nature of Robinson's discharge, the court of public opinion had reached its own verdict thanks to Parker's hit piece.

All the work that Robinson had done in giving exhibitions to almost three-quarters of a million troops was tarnished. To the *New York Daily Mirror*'s casual readers,

Robinson was a deserter, and probably a crooked boxer on top of it. One curious fall down a flight of stairs had knocked Robinson from his lofty perch; he was now arguably another low-life in a sport known for its corruption. Although such opinions were widespread, the incident with the man in the brown suit was the only time the AWOL issue was raised directly to Robinson's face. Still, Robinson knew then and there it would be a question that would haunt him for the rest of his life—as indeed it did. All Ray wanted was to box and get on with life. Yet it seemed that America wanted to rake him across the coals before he could rejoin the panoply of secular saints. It was up to Robinson, now, to make another choice: start over or throw in the towel.

Martin Luther King once told a story that puts this onerous, irrational responsibility in perspective. "Some time ago," he said, "one of the southern states adopted a new method of capital punishment. Poison gas supplanted the gallows. In its earliest stages, a microphone was placed inside the sealed death chamber so that scientific observers might hear the words of the dying prisoner. . . . The first victim was a young Negro. As the pellet dropped into the container, and gas curled upward, through the microphone came these words: "Save me, Joe Louis. Save me, Joe Louis. Save me, Joe Louis. . . . "

Some people pray to Jesus or Buddha or Allah. This young man prayed to a demigod of another sort: Joe Louis as a worker of miracles. It has been that way since the glad-iators fought for their lives in ancient Rome, and the implications have only multiplied over the years because athletes today are paid huge sums of money to play games the rest of us play for fun. The fact that some celebrity athletes really are worthy of emulation only muddies the water, but the title of "hero" goes with the person, not with the job description, the paycheck, or the headline.

NFL stars regularly get promoted to public legends in return for their on-the-field pains, but it took the events after September 11, 2001, to teach us that true heroism is a much deeper phenomenon than winning Super Bowls and championship belts.

Americans learned that the same firefighters who sometimes blocked their evening commute and police officers who occasionally annoyed them with traffic tickets can be as heroic as any soldier splashing ashore on D-Day. In the post–9/11 world, celebrity athletes, like movie stars and politicians, have learned soundly that a real hero's "uniform" isn't something to be taken off at the end of the day, when the final vote is counted, the last quarter is over, or the final bell has rung.

Pat Tillman is one athlete who met everyone's definition of heroism. Tillman's celebrity (at least beyond his Arizona fan base) was nowhere near the magnitude of Sugar Ray Robinson's. But even as a local celebrity, his life, and its ending, is a lesson for everyone.

"When he walked in, there was a tremendous amount of respect. I can see vividly in my mind each player shaking his hand, everyone saying thank you and touching his shoulder." This was Dave McGinnis, then head coach of the Arizona Cardinals, describing Sergeant Pat Tillman's visit to the locker room while on leave from a tour in Iraq. The Cardinals were playing the Seattle Seahawks, and Tillman, the former safety for the football team, was then stationed at nearby Fort Lewis, Washington. In 2002, Tillman, twenty-seven years old—a U.S. Army Ranger—was killed in Afghanistan during Operation Mountain Storm. Yet Tillman was no ordinary hero, even before he donned that army uniform.

Other NFL players have died in war. In World War II, 683 NFL players fought and 19 died, but most of today's fans don't remember their sacrifice. Although we've seen photographs of Joe Louis entertaining troops and marveled at baseball immortal Ted Williams in a flight suit, this is not the kind of service associated with sports heroes. Even Rocky Bleier, the gutsy Pittsburgh Steelers running back, did not "give up" a sports career to fight for his country: He was drafted by the army in 1968. Rocky was a hero because he played after suffering severe injuries from rifle and grenade wounds in Vietnam, but too many brave young troops came home from Vietnam and were ignored by those same fans.

Muhammad Ali's adventure with the military was another matter. Choosing to make a principled stand against the war in Vietnam and the disproportionate effect it was having on black recruits, he was pilloried in the press and by many former fans as a cowardly draft dodger hiding behind religious ideals. Today, with hindsight and a fuller view of Ali's character, as well as a greater understanding of the Vietnam War, public opinion has swayed in Ali's favor. He is remembered now as a larger-than-life hero who served his country in ways few people understood at the time. The man literally sacrificed millions of dollars to take, what he believed to be, the moral high ground.

Compare Ali now to the prewar Pat Tillman, a millionaire athlete for a new millennium who had an impressive career with the Arizona Cardinals. But football fans also appreciated Tillman as a good-looking, hard-working "surfer" who stayed true to his California upbringing, and they identified with him. He was no "loudmouth" outsider clawing his way to stardom—the contemporary impression of Ali during his incarnation as Cassius Clay; Tillman was a low-wattage celebrity. At only five foot ten inches, like Sugar Ray, he was defined not by unbelievable size but by quick wits, an unquenchable competitive spirit, and an unwavering work ethic. He was one of the last players selected in the final round of the 1998 NFL draft. Even the most sanguine Las Vegas odds makers would not have given him much chance for lasting in professional football. Not only did he make it; he was a leader for his team. He moved from his college linebacker position to star as a safety in the NFL. In 2000, he set a team record with 224 tackles.

to find valuable lessons in the positive and negative examples of those revered individuals. Two poignant examples of this come to mind. One was from baseball star Mickey Mantle who, nearing death, acknowledged years of alcohol abuse and advised his fans young and old: "Don't be like me." A second comes from the late 1980s, when the white heavyweight boxer Tommy Morrison—destined, apparently, for stardom when his talent was given exposure in the popular 1990 film *Rocky V* (Morrison played the role of Tommy Gunn)—was struck by the AIDS virus. He held a press conference acknowledging that he was HIV-positive, and said, "I ask that you no longer see me as a role model, but see me as an individual who had an opportunity to be a role model and blew it. Blew it with irresponsible, irrational, immature decisions that will one day cost me my life." Ironically, following an hour-long telephone conversation with the black basketball player Magic Johnson, Morrison proclaimed of his fellow HIV-positive athlete, "He's a great role model."

The expectations laid at the feet of anyone in the public eye can be staggering, and this seems to be especially true when those feet happen to be black. Even though black Americans represent only 12 percent of America's population, we are disproportionately represented in shocking images on television: young black men involved in crime, black families trapped in poverty, black people as helpless victims in natural disasters. The implicit message here is that because everything is so hopeless for this

12 percent minority, only a "superman" can save them, and that superman should be black.

For those who find themselves thrust into the spotlight merely because of the profession they chose, the results can be too much for one person to handle. When the basketball star Charles Barkley asserted on behalf of Nike that he was *not* a role model, most fans paused to think. The 1993 advertisement, made while Barkley was still playing and before he made such comments his trademark, said, "I am not a role model. I am not paid to be a role model. I am paid to wreak havoc on the basketball court. Parents should be role models. Just because I dunk a basketball doesn't mean I should raise your kids."

This is not your standard heroic script, but it makes a powerful and important point. Role modeling is not a perk of fame or a penalty clause in a multiyear contract. Some pro athletes are exceptional people; others are just regular people with exceptional talents. A person's ability to exploit a natural talent does not necessarily make that person worthy of emulation. Still, that's the reality now, and it began in the Sugar Ray era: When star athletes had role modeling forced upon them and their handlers and managers and intermediaries of all kinds—from journalists to product manufacturers—tried to cash in on the trend.

After he came back from a six-month suspension for going in to the stands and fighting with a fan who threw a cup at him, the troubled NBA star Ron Artest, true to his contrarian reputation, said, "I'm not trying to redo my image and please anybody. I'm going to continue to be myself, so I'm not trying to get Cheerio commercials or Coca-Cola commercials; I want to do a commercial in the 'hood." Most athletes are not so direct in their disavowal of heroics. Such protestations can begin to sound like the sigh of a jilted lover rather than the philosophical choice of a seasoned professional. Most comments on the topic by athletes fall somewhere short of the Barkley and Artest extremes. Most accept some level of obligation.

Those shocked by Barkley's bold assertions of self and Artest's disregard for white mainstream appeal need only look back a few decades for further examples of superstar athletes who did not have any desire to subvert their personalities or their pasts for the sake of their audience. Again, the extreme example of how *not* to cross over was provided by Jack Johnson.

Johnson proudly defied the social norms of the day. But to some blacks, he was a beacon who showed what could be achieved even when the pressures of white society were ignored. Many blacks saw Johnson's unconventional lifestyle and flamboyant behavior and admired it, even when they disagreed with the particulars—such as his penchant for interracial sexual relations. Some disliked Johnson the man, but they were in awe of Johnson the "superman," and through him they lived out their own secret dreams.

Joe Louis would later cross over after he defeated Max Schmeling. His victory over the German boxer at the height of Nazi claims of Aryan supremacy galvanized all Americans. This was one of the early instances in which nationality trumped race in America. Similarly, the track star Jesse Owens turned from black hero to American hero by defeating Hitler's finest athletes in the 1936 Olympics.

Although Owens and Louis still operated in the shadow of Jack Johnson, fan expectations had turned an important corner. To be sure, Johnson sold a lot of tickets to white fans, but mostly so they could see which *White Hope* would knock him out. Joe Louis was perhaps the first black boxer to win cheers simply for doing what he did best. In doing so, he imbued in white fans a better appreciation for the black culture that produced him. This was not an isolated phenomenon. White teenagers in the 1920s and '30s purchased "race music"—records and sheet music aimed primarily at black audiences—just as Motown and rap became popular to young whites in this era.

If a crossover black hero focused too much on race, even if he remained champion, he'd lose his mainstream audience. Jim Brown, the NFL Hall of Famer, learned this. But it wasn't as though he had any desire to cross over. Social activism is expensive in time, reputation, and money, and more than one athlete-activist faced potential ruin from involvement in political issues, especially those with a racial edge. Nobody doubted that Brown remained a fantastic athlete, but identification with highly charged racial or political issues reduced his market value.

Though he later fell into disrepute in the white community (and in much of the black, as well), O. J. Simpson was the first successful crossover athlete-celebrity in the television era in the 1960s and '70s. He was the first black athlete to be handsomely compensated for national endorsements, and he made a fine living in the late 1960s and '70s as spokesman for Hertz, Foster Grant, and Tree-Sweet orange juice. This was coupled with a relatively lucrative acting career.

Yet all this was mere prologue for someone many consider to be the greatest crossover athlete of all: Michael Jordan. So complete was Jordan's transition, critics say, that he withheld his support from Harvey Gantt in the black candidate's 1990 senatorial campaign against Jesse Helms in North Carolina. Helms had never been a friend to black voters. Many in the black community wondered why Jordan simply didn't step up and "support a brotha."

Jordan explained on *60 Minutes* and elsewhere that he couldn't do everything that everyone expected of him. To be fair, there are reports that Jordan made a financial contribution to Gantt. But that's pretty tepid stuff compared to the costly political stances of John Carlos and Tommie Smith with the black-gloved salute on the 1968 Olympics victory stand, and Jim Brown's vigilant outspokenness and black economic empowerment activity at the height of his playing career. Jordan's endorsement of a fellow black would have put Gantt on the political map and done inestimable service to black interests not only in the South but also in the nation.

Much of the debate about the social obligations of black superstars currently focuses on Tiger Woods. Critics ask, "Tiger, why don't you speak up about the absence of women and people of color in all those fancy country clubs and prestigious tournaments?"

We don't hear much in reply from Tiger, but here are two persuasive explanations. First, Martha Burk—a recent figure in "female desegregation"—may not have struck Tiger as the kind of dynamic leader needed to end gender, religious, and racial bias at private country clubs. Even if he had a strong emotional, as well as intellectual and moral, interest in the issue, there was not at that time a national movement mandated to bring down these clubs "by any means necessary." In fact, none of the other members of the PGA felt strongly enough about Burke to join a boycott.

Remember, those currently pushing athletes hardest to be more socially and politically active tend to be those who came of age politically in the 1960s, when activism was fashionable, though not always rewarded. The list of black sports activists begins with the usual suspects—Ali, Jim Brown, John Carlos, and Tommie Smith—and continues to late-blooming heroes such as Arthur Ashe, who took on South African apartheid and the AIDS pandemic. But in those days, athlete-activists were not leaders of great movements; they were influential followers. From strategic planning to grassroots get-out-the-vote-and-protest campaigns, they deferred real leadership to more politically savvy icons such as Martin Luther King, Malcolm X, and a legion of Vietnam/Cold War critics from Hollywood and the media. Outside of the sports context, Harry Belafonte, Dick Gregory, Jane Fonda, and others all followed strong leaders in the movements they joined but didn't create. Today, there are few clearly defined movements, and even fewer charismatic personalities to lead them.

Tiger also represents a new kind of role model: a quieter celebrity who makes the world a better place simply by *insisting* that he be a part of it. His Stanford education and supportive parents may be anomalous to many who would follow in his footsteps; but in their own way, Tiger and others show that oppression is *not* the natural condition for anyone. Today's young people, black and white, are too busy getting on with their lives to watch reruns of *Eyes on the Prize*. To boomers and their parents, this sounds a lot like apathy; but on closer inspection, it suggests a fundamental shift in the way young people look at themselves and the traits they look for in heroes. To paraphrase a popular Oldsmobile ad, *this is not your father's movement*.

Although Robinson came of age as a public figure when speaking out on race was even less welcome than the time Jim Brown did it, he did have interactions while in the military through which he displayed a level of social activism. The best-known instance was his position of not giving boxing exhibitions unless the events were attended by white soldiers as well as black. His insistence on an integrated audience was a bold stance in that era because the military had not yet been integrated by the federal government.

For whatever reason, political progress or the dearth of leaders, the imperative for athlete activism has subsided. The tumult of the 1960s is long in the past. Some of this deemphasis of social issues is undoubtedly generational. The story of Kellen Winslow Jr. and his father (the archetypal tight end of the 1980s, Kellen Winslow Sr.) sheds a bright light on this generation gap. Kellen Sr. was not even a teenager when he saw John Carlos and Tommie Smith in Mexico City raise their fists on the victory stand. But their message never left him. In his 1995 National Football League Hall of Fame induction speech, many old timers wanted to crawl under their chairs in their yellow blazers as he urged affirmative action in the league front offices and elsewhere. He wanted athletes to compel increased diversity in sports front offices, just as they had done on the field. Little did he know that his son, Kellen Jr., would be given just that opportunity half a decade later.

The Winslow plan was simple, though Kellen Sr. never had a chance to implement it as a player in the pre-free agency days. "Make a public statement," he said, "that the organization . . . must have people that look like me in positions of power."

The intergenerational saga played itself out on national television. The Winslows had agreed to sign a National Letter of Intent on the Fox Sports Net football television show, for which Kellen Sr. provided the commentary. This letter is signed by high school athletes to declare to the world where they will be going to college. During the broadcast, it became clear that father and son had not yet come to an agreement. They announced there would be a delay in their decision.

"I told him to take a look around," Kellen Sr. said, "thumb through the media guides and see how far you have to turn before you get to a person of color. And if you don't see people that look like you, there's a problem. There has to be some reason behind it."

Kellen Sr. was called a lot of things, including racist, for attempting to raise his son's consciousness about the realities of front-office bias. All he was really trying to be was a good father. Kellen, the son, had been spared the crucible through which his father had passed. Life has been good for Kellen Jr., but it still held pitfalls for the unwary.

The compromise between father and son was Miami. The "U" did not have a black head coach, but the receivers' coach was black, and that had a direct impact on the younger Kellen's career decision. The Winslow family action at the beginning of this millenium informed the institutions that they passed on of their mistake. Dad was concerned about the racial composition of your athletic department, the Winslow actions were telling them, and whether his son was concerned or not, he did not end up coming to your institution. If only for a moment, the college sports world had been given something to contemplate.

But the Kellen Winslow story and affirmative action were not part of Robinson's world. Sugar Ray Robinson was no Pat Tillman, who was a true hero but a minor celebrity. Sugar Ray was also no Ted Williams, who served in two wars and went on to bat .400. Tillman and Williams are certified war heroes—and were seemingly heroic at whatever task they undertook. Robinson was a different kind of celebrity. He was a crossover who managed to keep one foot in two boats; and his ability to shift his balance between them, whenever the situation required it, led directly to the Tiger Woodses and Michael Jordans of today. Tillman chose not to be a vocal social activist. He rejected opportunities to speak about why he enlisted and the politics that inspired him to do so. To him, public service was its own justification and reward. He did not feel the need to convince others of the rightness of his cause. He would lead by example or not at all. Maybe his reputation would have been greater, his legacy more powerful, if he had articulated his views. But that was not his way. Every celebrity athlete has his own style, and the best ones know their limitations.

Robinson was haunted by the "desertion story" for the rest of his life. Ten years after his June 1944 discharge from the army, in May 1954, the House of Representatives Armed Services Subcommittee on alleged "coddling" of athletes raised the issue again. Another lesson for today's athletes. Ray himself tried to diffuse the matter, but talking about it seemed to do more harm than good. One official making reference to the event said that Robinson had "jumped ship." With childlike enthusiasm, Robinson snapped back that it was impossible because he was "never on a ship." He then personalized the accusations: "That's a hurting thing, man . . . I have a son and this is pretty low kind of fighting." He concluded by playing the race card, saying that if he were a black deserter there would have been no honorable discharge. "I went where they sent me in the Army. A fellow of my color doesn't buck them."

Years later W. C. Heinz, in that 1970s interview mentioned earlier, did get a bit more unexpected information from Robinson. When Heinz mentioned to Ray that he had worked as a correspondent in World War II, Robinson asked, "How come we didn't meet over there?" He went on, "We were over there, Joe Louis and I, we had a troupe, and we boxed in the ETO [European Theater of Operations] and everything." Heinz did not press. He wrote that Robinson was a man "who has his own illusions about his life, as do we all, about the way he wishes it had been, and there is little if any harm, although some sadness, in that now."

Sugar Ray was no O. J. Simpson (pre-white Bronco) or Michael Jordan. Although he was able to cross over the racial divide, he still nurtured and cherished the black aspirations of his day. He was no Muhammad Ali, Jim Brown, John Carlos, Tommie Smith, or Arthur Ashe, but those impressive figures might not have existed—or enjoyed their opportunities—without the trail Ray Robinson blazed. He was not a hero in the classical sense, but few athlete-celebrities are. He was the key transition link to their rarified level of athletic celebrity and their opportunity to be heroes, activists, and role models.

CHAPTER FOUR

STYLE

It's the second round of Ray Robinson's December 20, 1946, welterweight title bout with Tommy Bell. The first round was typical and by-the-book: Sugar Ray is superior. But the second round begins a little differently. Tommy rings Ray's bell with a bone-jarring uppercut, and Ray staggers back, trying to shake off the black lights. According to Muhammad Ali: "They say when you get hit and hurt bad you see black lights—the black lights of unconsciousness." Ray goes down.

Bell and Robinson are fighting for the welterweight title vacated by Marty Servo earlier in the year. The boxing public all but demanded this fight. The matchmakers finally had to give Robinson a title shot regardless of his arrogance, race, and failure to cooperate with the mob.

Bell entered the bout against Robinson as a 1-5 under-dog, a good bet if Bell has a lucky day, and his luck seems to be turning. He knows he has to make quick work of Robinson: Knock him down early and keep him there. If it came down to a decision, Robinson would take the fight. His style and skills made it difficult for anyone to beat him on points. Although Ray never held the title, most experts considered him the best welterweight in the field. His only loss in seventy-five fights had been to Jake La Motta, and Bell was not in La Motta's class. At this point Robinson was viewed as the uncrowned champ.

After the knockdown, Robinson climbs back to one knee. His head clears and he hears the "seven" count. Robinson lurches up directly into a buzz saw of Bell's box-ing gloves—combinations that Robinson wasn't expect-ing. Bell is going for a knockout. Robinson ducks and weaves, backs off, blocks some blows, and buys some time. After a long half minute, he begins dancing, jabbing, and countering. He's back on offense. His corner men shout advice. Ray hears half of it. Their voices are more reassur-ing than instructive. Ray really doesn't need instruction. He knows what he has to do.

The second round ends, then the third. Bell is aggres-sive and Ray can't build momentum. Finally, in the fourth round, Bell, getting tired and frustrated, slips and falls. He gets up quickly, goes on the attack, and falls again. Ray never lays a glove on him. He gets up and Ray goes back to work. The fifth round ends, and the next two rounds are relatively uneventful. Neither fighter can break out. Though Ray looks confident, he still hasn't taken control of the fight. In the eighth round, Bell slips down yet again. So far, gravity is ahead on points. The ninth and tenth rounds come and go. In the eleventh, Ray catches the exhausted Bell with a strong left hook followed by a blistering right cross. Bell goes down. The count goes up to eight before Bell staggers back to his feet.

The final rounds give the 15,670 fans in the stands the show they expected. It is Robinson dominating. Even so, there is a grumble when he wins a unanimous decision: Bell had scored his share of points, especially in the early going. But the longer the fight went on, the more Robinson took command. Now he finally had what his soaring reputation long demanded: a title to match his fame. The next decade belonged to him.

"There goes Sugar Ray!"

Fingers point at the flamingo-pink Cadillac as it tools down 125th Street on the way to Robinson's personal "business district." Today, Ray rides alone. His camel-hair coat is laid neatly in the back seat, and his crisply snapped gray fedora sits on the passenger seat beside him, ready for action. There's an old saying: Peacocks strut because they can't fly. Sugar Ray was that rarest of birds: a flying peacock full of flash, feathers, and fight.

He stops his car below a neon sign. It glows bright pink, even though it's late afternoon and the sun is still shining. It says *Sugar Ray's*. Some cronies hanging around out front amble curbside to receive him. Others emerge from the bar and do the same.

"Hey, old buddy," Ray extends his universal greeting. He slaps five and shakes hands as the usual crowd gathers around the Cadillac, the outdoor meeting place.

The car's pink tone reminded many of a high-class lady's nail polish. If the Cadillac got a scratch, you could almost imagine Sugar Ray reaching into his wife, Edna Mae's, purse to perform a quick touch up. That particular shade was hard enough to find—for cars or for nail polish—but Robinson had a way of getting what he wanted. He used to buy blue Buicks. The idea of a pink Caddy came to him while he was admiring the flamingos on the infield of the Hialeah racetrack in Florida, and took root when he saw the same color on the snazzy tie of boxer Willie Pep's manager.

Pep's manager was not Robinson's sole style influence. At some point, early on, Robinson decided that style was important. His father was a stylish dresser, at least when he could afford to be. But that was a distant memory. The wheels may have been set in motion by Robinson's first manager, Curt Horrmann, the man who influenced him to begin consuming late-night steaks, the man who drove a big maroon Packard and wore tailored British suits. A sense of style was part of Robinson's makeup.

The chrome on the Cadillac dazzled the eyes, even on a cloudy day. 1950s luxury models were made, unlike today's half-plastic cars, with heavy chrome: half for safety, all for show. The tires had "*gangsta* whitewalls": white rubber on the sidewalls a full four inches wide. Peacocks like to be noticed.

Athletes today may have vanity plates (Ray had that too, "27 RR"), but their fame-mobiles might as well belong to stockbrokers. Although a few athletes before Robinson had cars to trumpet their arrival, Robinson's—particularly with the outrageous color—raised the bar. There weren't a lot of pink luxury cars cruising the streets of Harlem, so this one attracted attention. Hanging out around a cool car was a favorite pastime amongst the locals.

Ray talked about that special car in his autobiography. "When my car arrived," he wrote, "it was not only exclusive, it was a symbol. When people think they recognize a celebrity, they hesitate a moment. But when they saw me in that car, they didn't have to hesitate. They knew. There was only one like it—Sugar Ray's pink Cadillac featuring the black convertible top. But to me it was always more than pink, it was flamingo pink. And first the car was an even bigger attraction than I was. Its paint job made it the most famous car in the world."

He also referred to his car as the "Hope Diamond" of Harlem: partly because it was such a jewel, partly because of the hope its very existence—*his* career—gave the community. Successful athletes today rarely wax so poetically about their vehicles—even the Gulfstream jets many of them own. Ray's Cadillac, on the other hand, was known around the world. Recently, one of the guests at a lunch in Paris said, "My great grandmother rented an apartment to Sugar Ray Robinson." Then, in almost the same breath he said, "Oh—she really loved that pink Cadillac! What a beauty it must have been."

In Robinson's era, another soon-to-be celebrity had Cadillac dreams. Writing that he had owned nothing as a kid, he reflected on his aspirations: "When you're a kid, you don't think much about it. You don't go around feeling sorry for yourself. . . . You wonder what it would be like to have all the dough you wanted and drive around in a Cadillac . . . and you dream that when you grow up that's how it's going to be." This was Sugar Ray's long time rival, Jake La Motta. The Cadillac continued to be a sign of success until European cars began to dominate the market. This was reflected in Jim Brown's life as well: "Before I came to the Browns, none of the players owned Cadillacs." Brown chose to buy one even though there was a rule stipulating that players could not own Cadillacs. "But I was not a Ford Fairlane type guy. Rookie year, I purchased a Cadillac convertible. It was light purple and white." Ironically, the Cadillac is again a showcase vehicle with athletes and entertainers, this time in the SUV incarnation, the Escalade.

Next door to *Sugar Ray's* at 2076 7th Avenue was *Ray Robinson Enterprises*, headquarters of the entire Robinson

empire. His businesses on the block included George Gainford's Golden Glovers Barber Shop, Edna Mae's Lingerie
Shop, and Sugar Ray's Quality Cleaners. Standing in front
of both buildings were a dozen black men dressed in felt
hats and overcoats. They weren't gangsters or undertakers;
that's just the way you dressed as a self-respecting man in
the mid-twentieth century, even in impoverished Harlem.
You wore a suit when you took a train or an airliner. Ladies
wore hats and gloves for a night on the town. The styles
were conservative; clothing was mainly gray, black, or
beige, and gentlemen's hats had a narrow black band that
matched their ties. With that semiofficial dress code came
a kind of civility to strangers that also is long gone.

Sugar Ray's bar was an inviting place. Robinson wanted
it that way. At night, the lighting was reminiscent of the
Las Vegas strip or, more locally, Times Square. The black
canopy over the entrance was held up by metal poles. The
arch of that awning displayed the name *Sugar Ray's* in gold
letters. It was an entrance that would have looked as much
at home on the Champs Elysées in Paris as in Harlem.

The amiable crowd of black men hanging curbside with
Robinson and his Cadillac, and the other celebrities who
came and went, was a regular feature of *Sugar Ray's Café*
throughout the 1950s. When the gathering got too big
and blocked the sidewalk, or drive-by gawkers clogged the
street, police officers just looked the other way.

The breadth and depth of Robinson's success was enormous. He associated with political powers such as Mayor

Impellitteri and Walter Winchell. Inside *Sugar Ray's Café*, patrons ran into celebrities such as Jackie Gleason, Frank Sinatra, and Nat King Cole, as well as big-time boxers and big-league athletes from other sports. It was a place to see and be seen, and Ray did his best to make sure that everyone, even people like that little man in the brown suit, got a chance.

For white patrons, coming to *Sugar Ray's* exemplified what Norman Mailer wrote about in his 1957 essay *The White Negro*. Mailer saw the embrace of black culture by whites as their way of dealing with death. According to Mailer, whites thought that by associating themselves with the black's survivor culture, by learning to live a vibrant life in the face of daily mortal danger, they would become happier, more durable people. The specter of death was a product of the times. The Cold War rose to a boil in Korea, and school children everywhere were taught the mantra of "duck and cover" to ward off the atomic bomb. Regardless of the reason, this white "embrace" of black culture was most evidenced in the white pursuit of jazz. Before World War II, "hot jazz," the bouncy descendant of Harlem stride and New Orleans Dixieland, dominated popular music and led to the big band era. After the war, "cool jazz" took over: the more cerebral, yet equally soulful, music of Charlie Parker and Miles Davis. Mailer extrapolated this trend to other aspects of American culture. Being black was *hip* and *cool*.

Going to Harlem, being seen at *Sugar Ray's Café*, being seen with Sugar Ray, were all *cool*. *Sugar Ray's Café* provided both literal and figurative soul food for those who ventured uptown to get a taste of this new phenomenon.

Beyond those in the café and Harlem circle, among those still seeking clues to what *coolness* was all about—in an age before cable television networks, satellite broadcasts, tabloid journalism, and hardcore paparazzi—Robinson, though famous, was still something of an enigma. He knew that, and characteristically used it to his advantage. The public could admire the Champ in the ring or enjoy his celebrity outside it—it didn't make any difference to Ray. He seemed to understand that each fan projected his own image onto this "character" called Sugar Ray. This was not about role modeling; it was about *style*.

In this respect, the pink Cadillac was only the tip of the iceberg. Sugar Ray was always impeccably dressed. If he was not in the ring or training, he wore tailored suits, a tuxedo, a camel-hair overcoat, or a colorful knit shirt. This is one reason why more than a few of those die-hard Sugar Ray fans shook their heads on that final farewell evening at the Garden. Unless Sugar Ray came to knock you out, he dressed like a man of taste and prosperity.

As Michael Jordan matured in the NBA, he came to present a similar brand of Robinson cool. Like Robinson, Jordan let his fans take their choice between personas: the man in the ring (or on the court) and the man on the

street, in the club or at a restaurant, and each had a definite "uniform." Fans came to care about what their idols
were wearing, and they began to emulate what they admired. This strategy for shaping celebrity is no accident.
Others have tried it and failed. Shannon Sharpe, Deion
Sanders, Michael Irvin, and Magic Johnson take it all a
bit too far with one too many buttons or an overload of
hand-stitched details on their suits. The line between
high style and bad taste is sometimes narrow; only the
exceptional individual knows where that border is.

The point to remember is that *fashion* is not the same
as style. Many modern athletes follow the fashion of their
young fans by bopping around with headphones, hiding
inside a hoodie, or munching on an energy bar and wash-
ing it down with a can of soda. Meanwhile, the cameras
click. Those photos, they'll discover later in their careers,
will date them faster than a birth certificate. Fashion is
fickle. Style lasts.

Cool is perhaps the ultimate expression of style, although it is sometimes masked by fashion. That's why so
many people who say they "want to be cool, like so-and-
so" become mere parodies of the genuine article. Miles
Davis knew his music was cool, but his image as a celebrity
(beyond a handful of connoisseurs) was lacking. Interest-
ingly, he looked to Sugar Ray for his model.

"In 1954 he was the most important thing in my life
besides music," Davis told his biographer, Quincy Troupe.

"I found myself acting like him, you know, everything. Even taking on his arrogant attitude. Ray was cold and he was the best and was everything I wanted to be in 1954." Davis, like many, interpreted Ray's combination of self-confidence and self-control as arrogance and equated it with cool. Ray always had a smile and a wave and a "How you doin,' old buddy?" for everyone, but he transcended many of the troubles around him, and that set him apart from others. If that was arrogance, it was contagious and everyone wanted to be infected.

During this era of cool, Robinson fought Rocky Graziano, one of the most lasting names of the day. They met in the ring on April 16, 1952, in Chicago. Both boxers were thirty years old. This was seven years after Graziano shouted following a victory, "Get me Robinson!"

Robinson, in white trunks, dances out of his corner at the ring of the bell. Rocky, wearing black, charges to center ring and lets loose a roundhouse left. Robinson, watching for Graziano's powerful right, gets suckered and is tagged by the left. He falls forward into a clinch—a textbook recovery that sets the tone for the early rounds. Robinson jabs back aggressively, giving Graziano a taste of his own left hook. Graziano falls back to the ropes. Ray follows and they clinch again. Graziano begins throwing rabbit punches. The crowd boos and referee Tommy Gilmore warns him to stop. They break.

Robinson attacks immediately. Graziano tries to counterpunch, but his opponent is quicker and smarter. Robinson now shows fans and experts a curious side of his game. He was always an aggressive fighter, but now he is taking risks: inviting punches that would put any boxer, including Robinson, down for the count. Robinson knows that if he doesn't give an experienced boxer like Graziano an apparent opening, the bout will degenerate into a grueling marathon. That's how boxers get worn out. Even worse, it makes for a poor show, and Sugar Ray, by now, has become synonymous with showmanship. By inviting his opponent to attack before he's ready—get excited and greedy and overextend himself—he sets the stage for a quick, clean "kill."

Again, mid-round, following a series of lightning combinations that score on Graziano, Robinson clinches and drives him to his corner. Graziano rabbit punches again—a sign of frustration—and again he is warned.

Both fighters relax and try to size each other up. With a minute remaining in the round, Graziano lunges with the left again, but it's only a glancing blow. Robinson dances away unharmed. Graziano fights like a cobra: He hunches over, leans forward, weaves his head hypnotically. Ray realizes that this is Rocky's own way of inviting an impetuous attack. It's not an open taunt—Ray's own ploy is more subtle—but the intention is the same.

With thirty seconds left in the round, Graziano catches Robinson on the chin. Ray counters aggressively and drives

Graziano into a corner. At the end of the first, Robinson has Rocky on the ropes, wilting under a flurry of punches. Graziano, clearly no beginner, finds a way out. Nonetheless, to the odds-makers, Robinson is looking more and more like the favorite who started the fight. Years later, Graziano said that he really thought he could knock Robinson out, at least after that first round.

In round two, the boxers advance to center ring. The first shot of adrenaline has subsided and there's a bit more pacing in this round. Sugar Ray backs off his toes and throws a few punches flat-footed. The blistering exchanges of round one have visibly fatigued both boxers. The circling continues. They exchange blows, but neither fighter gains an advantage. It's clear to most observers that Graziano is looking for the knockout blow. He knows he can't go fifteen rounds with Sugar Ray. Robinson later said his plan was to "not get hit by that right," but he had invited such attacks in the first round in hopes of settling things fast. Graziano would not take the bait. Caution begins to reign.

Eventually, Robinson's jabs begin to get through. Graziano's head snaps back. He replies in kind, and both fighters score points. As the bell sounds, Graziano lands one last, solid left. Ray isn't hurt, but he looks surprised. Graziano hops back to his corner with a renewed surge of confidence.

In the third round, they meet again at center ring. Rocky fails to follow up on the blow that ended the last round. He knows how dangerous Ray is once he has been tagged. He appears to have shifted his strategy and is now going for points, and he seems to believe he can go fifteen rounds; scores for the bout so far are very close, with Robinson having a slight lead on all cards. After another combination, Graziano reaches down to adjust his trunks, a classic sign of a fighter playing for time, of a fight-plan coming unraveled.

Graziano perseveres. Having abandoned his hope for a knockout, he knows he has to score points, and do so while his tiring legs and arms can still protect him from Robinson's speed and endurance. Unfortunately for Graziano, Robinson seems disinclined to close and trade punches. Two minutes into the round, Graziano sees an apparent advantage and takes it. It is the trap Robinson had set, but his rapid counterattack misfires. Still, he drives Rocky into the ropes, closing a series of combinations with a right to the jaw that leaves Graziano stunned. For an instant, the Champ relaxes. It is an instant too long. Graziano lashes out with a right to Ray's jaw and Robinson goes down. The referee moves in as Robinson regains one knee. Graziano edges toward a neutral corner. Within seconds, Robinson is up. With no mandatory eight count (the fight is in Illinois, not New York), the referee wipes off Robinson's gloves and the fight resumes.

Robinson now "gets on his scooter." Graziano isn't going to fall from a sucker punch, and he is willing to go for points, so Ray has to reassess his strategy. To give himself time, and to help wear Rocky out, Ray backpedals and circles, taking a tour of the ring. Graziano follows like an old bulldog. Robinson jabs with his left as he moves backward. Most of the punches connect. Years later, an aging Joe Louis said that Sugar Ray was the one fighter who could punch just as hard moving backward as forward.

Robinson lands a powerful right to the jaw. The crowd is on its feet. He then delivers a lightning combination and Rocky's mouth guard flies out. The challenger drops like a stone.

Robinson turns and walks to the neutral corner like a bullfighter who knows a beast is finished. Graziano does not get up. The Champ is still the Champ. Like so many challengers that Robinson fought—La Motta, Basilio, Fullmer—Rocky wants to keep going even after he is down and out. All he can do is stare in disbelief. He knows he's supposed to get up, but for those first few seconds all he can see are those black lights. The referee counts Graziano out. He looks directly at the timekeeper and they count in unison, right hands raised then coming down showing the same number of fingers.

Rocky's cornermen rush out. As Robinson is toweled down in center ring, Rocky punches the ropes in anger. If this were a street fight, it wouldn't be over. That's why professional boxing has rules. In the end he collects himself, congratulates Robinson, and holds the Champ's arm up in victory. Sugar Ray graces him—and the crowd—with that famous smile.

Graziano would recover from this defeat and fight once more before leaving boxing for standup comedy. Later, he recorded a comedy album, *The Maharishi Yogurt*, and wrote a book about his life, *Somebody Up There Likes Me*, which became a motion picture. Graziano also carried with him a dishonorable discharge from the army, but that seemed to have little impact on *his* popularity.

This breathtaking victory over a successful, popular boxer raised Robinson's fame to greater heights. He had beaten La Motta, held the title, and now he had beaten Graziano. For most fighters, that would have been enough; but remember, life inside the ring was only one-half of *being* Sugar Ray. The other half was cultivating a celebrity image, and that meant transforming each new success into another aspect of his personal style.

Sugar Ray's brand of style was accessible and universal; each victory added to his patina of cool. It wasn't just superficial; the man inside the clothing made the difference. Sugar Ray, like Michael Jordan, had a winning smile and used it appropriately. Both their complexions were unmistakably black and perfect; metaphorically speaking (Jordan, after all, shaved his head), neither appeared in public with a hair out of place. Being Sugar Ray or Michael Jordan meant taking care of yourself and caring what others thought about you—and respecting that stylistic obligation.

Now consider Muhammad Ali, a self-confessed heir, and student, of Sugar Ray's; he was never a fashion plate. Still, Ali had a keen awareness of style; or, at a minimum, he knew the value of maintaining a pleasing appearance. After bouts, as the broadcaster Howard Cosell came into the ring to do one of their famous postfight interviews, Ali was often seen running a mid-sized cake-cutter comb, handed to him by Bundini Brown, through his short afro, making an attempt, at least, to freshen up for the camera. But hair and clothes were certainly not the essence of Ali's style.

In many circumstances, the attire says much about the attired. In 2005, Mike Nolan became coach of the San Francisco 49ers and wanted to wear a suit and tie on the sidelines. He hoped that an injection of formality and class would further polish the image of the NFL, which had been tarnished by showboating and poor sportsmanship.

Nolan's father, Dick Nolan, who coached the 49ers in the 1960s, was one of the last to patrol the NFL sidelines in a business suit. When Mike Nolan told Brian McCarthy, an NFL executive, about his plan, McCarthy paled. He pointed out that the league's corporate sponsorship contract stipulated that coaches wear only team-issued apparel. At the time, Reebok held the exclusive license to provide on-field and sideline apparel for all NFL teams, and suits and ties were not in the Reebok catalog. ESPN's *Pardon the Interruption* host Mike Wilbon joked, "The NFL powers look exceptionally stupid and petty for basically saying, 'We'd rather a guy look like a homeless man like [New England Patriots' coach Bill] Belichick than a man wearing a suit and tie representing his franchise and his league."

The demise of the old NFL suit-and-tie era also coincided with the end of Sugar Ray's reign. Television presented football in the style of Vince Lombardi, Paul Brown, and Hank Stram. Suits were in fashion. Tom Landry of the Dallas Cowboys was the last holdout of the suit-and-tie era, but the imperial decree remains.

The NFL's corporate obligations seemingly mandated casual attire on the sidelines, but the NBA controversially took steps to roll back the tide of informality. The league issued a memo dictating how players dress in settings where they are deemed to represent the league. The October 17, 2005, memo sent to NBA players from the commissioner's office announced that they are "required to wear *Business Casual* attire whenever they are engaged in team or league business." The "business casual" definition prohibited sleeveless shirts, T-shirts, jerseys, headgear "of any kind," chains, pendants, and medallions.

Although the NBA Player's Association agreed to it—such is the brotherhood between big businesses—not all were pleased with the rule. Dissenters were concerned about having their right of choice stripped away. More directly, many inside and outside the game felt that the new policy was racist. Its biggest impact was on young black males in the league. Boston Celtic star, Paul Pierce, delivered what may be the most thoughtful and savvy analysis of the dress code: "Every player should have a feel of how they market their own selves. If you don't feel like you have to wear a coat and tie, you shouldn't have to."

Pierce, a veteran, clearly considered himself an adult who needed no help in dressing himself—certainly not by David Stern, the league commissioner. "Every player is different in their own way, just like they are on the court. You look at these artists, these actors, these movie stars, they're entertainers and they have their own sense of style. It's the same with what we do. We're an industry. We should be able to dress the way we feel. This is more a freestyle, freelance business, just like acting. If you want to market yourself a certain way by the way you dress, I feel you should be allowed to."

Although Pierce makes a lot of sense, one must consider the dynamics of the employer/employee relationship. If IBM pays big salaries and requires its white-collar staff to wear white shirts and ties shouldn't a company that pays even more be able to protect its corporate interests by insisting that employees present themselves in a way that helps its image? No question that it is over-reaching to tell a grown man how to dress—but that's the current corporate dynamic.

Allen Iverson had his own issues with the NBA dress code. "I feel like if they want us to dress a certain way, they should pay for our clothes," he told a reporter querying him about the 2005 NBA dress code. Again, that appears to be a false step for most athletes. With this comment, Iverson broke one of the unwritten rules of the modern era: Don't make any comment that implies you don't appreciate how much more money you make than *everyman*. Unaware of his faux pas, Iverson went on to condemn the impact that league rules can have on individual style: "It's tough, man, knowing that all of a sudden you have to have a dress code out of nowhere. I don't think that's going to help the image of the league at all. . . . It kind of makes it fake. The whole thing is fake."

Image and commerce are the forces at odds in all these debates about clothing and personal style. Protecting the image of the NBA is tantamount to pleasing longtime fans and keeping an open channel between their wallets and the league's coffers. This age-old formula has become further complicated because the live gate is more and more the concern of corporate America. This is certainly true of the most prized customers of all organized sports: companies that invest in luxury suites. In the corporate culture of those "best customers," a dress-code mentality still rules, whether that code is dictated by tradition or by a paragraph in a licensing contract.

There is a battle between the right of a league to set its own image versus the right of individual players to define theirs. In the background of this conflict is one about safeguarding profits—whether in the form of league-wide contracts with Reebok or in individual endorsement opportunities. Style counts in professional sports. It can count against the bottom line and as a bargaining chip between a league and its employees.

Fashion, cars, personal appearance, and finally homes. As athletes increasingly find their attire and behavior off the field proscribed, the last outpost of their style is often the home. The Robinson home was featured in *Ebony* magazine in June 1953. The article ran while Sugar Ray was in the throws of his post-Maxim *I am now an entertainer* retirement. At this point, he was referred to as an "entertainer," but the boxer—and the Champ—was never far from the surface.

Certainly, by today's standards, his was a modest home. "This is my dream house," Robinson told *Ebony*, "the kind of home I've wanted all of my life." It was a simple four-story brick house: a ten-room home in the Riverdale section of the Bronx. A couple of flowering trellises constituted the landscaping. Concrete steps led to an unimposing front door, which was located on the side of the house. The home was set back from the curb, maybe ten feet—hardly a Hamptons-type circular driveway.

The interior bore the distinctive marks of its owner. Decoration was the key. The Robinsons had a seven-foot-diameter circular bed. *Ebony* called the kitchen "the finest example of the most modern American kitchen." The home also featured a sunlit solarium furnished with bamboo furniture. Today, that strikes one as more Pier 1 than Neiman Marcus. The master bedroom was air conditioned, there was a bar on the fourth floor, and the home had an intercom.

This home was the cover story of a magazine that then had a circulation of more than five hundred thousand. On the front page was Ray, his wife Edna Mae, and their son, the three sitting together on a burgundy velvet sofa. The cover teaser was, "Sugar Ray's Dream House," followed by a second lead story, "My Mother Was a Man."

One star who learned the importance of creating a unique space for oneself in the Robinson vein was Wilt Chamberlain. Chamberlain's preferred name was "the Dipper"—at least that's what they called him when he was growing up in Philadelphia. The name had nothing to do with basketball; he was so tall he had to dip to enter door wells and everywhere else to avoid bumping his head. He did not like "Wilt the Stilt," which in his mind had an artificial quality about it. Style is genuine, or it is nothing at all.

Chamberlain would have been one of the early stars of MTV's *Cribs* had the show existed in the 1960s and 1970s. Chamberlain, who grew up in Philadelphia and spent plenty of time in New York City, was probably influenced by Robinson, who boxed regularly in New York and Philadelphia. Chamberlain's house, once he reached stardom, reflected the style of money. It had a name—"Ursa Major"—after the constellation that contains the Big Dipper. The design, with its interlocking equilateral triangles, was reminiscent of Frank Lloyd Wright. The house had a panoramic view, and when the Los Angeles smog did not obscure the sights, the Pacific Ocean was visible all the way to Catalina Island. The *Cribs* style features an eight-by-nine-foot bed, a gold-laced marble bath tub, a bedspread made of seventeen thousand Arctic wolf noses, and a retractable ceiling that allowed the Dipper and his guest to view the stars. Style needn't be practical, but it has to be memorable.

Chamberlain may or may not have been emulating Robinson, and certainly he took his architectural cues from Wright, but no one dictated style to Robinson. He developed his own. Boxing—more than virtually any other sport—allows for that level of individuality. Unfortunately, the looseness of the sport also allows for so much abuse. Connecting with his public was in his genes. Sugar Ray did more than embody the idea of cool: he made it a marketable product.

CHAPTER FIVE

RIVALRIES

On Valentine's Day, 1951, more than 14,800 seats had been sold for what some people hoped would be Sugar Ray Robinson's last stand. Ray was about to meet his nemesis—the burr of his boxing career. If Jake La Motta wanted anything that night, it was to be known the next morning as the man who defeated Sugar Ray Robinson twice.

The two boxers first fought in 1942. Robinson won that meeting. In the second brawl with La Motta, on February 5, 1943, he literally knocked Robinson out of the ring, with a right slamming into his body and a solid follow-up shot to his head, between the first and second ropes. Robinson made it back in the ring for a full nine count, but lost the ten-rounder on a decision. Before that bout, La Motta was a "prelim" fighter, rarely a headliner.

La Motta would receive *The Ring* magazine's Fighter of the Year award for 1943 largely because he had been the first to knock off Robinson. Now Sugar Ray had won eighty-two consecutive fights since suffering what was up to then his only loss. Still, La Motta's victory planted the seed in fans' minds that if he beat Sugar Ray once, he just might do it again, a threat Robinson himself took seriously. The 18,930 spectators at that earlier Detroit fight would see—for the first time—a boxer who would keep coming in on Robinson with no fear.

The first fight whiff of equality—and after all it was only a whiff—is what made this rivalry so compelling: Either side could win on any given day. When one athlete wins all the time, it's not a rivalry. It lacks the requisite suspense. Although Ray was ultimately victorious in all but one of their six meetings, none was a cakewalk. That La Motta became Robinson's toughest opponent obstructs the chasm between their respective careers. La Motta ended his career after 106 fights, winning 83–30 by a knockout—and losing 23, five of which were to Robinson. Compare this to Robinson's 202 lifetime bouts. If each fight takes a little bit out of you, such longevity is astonishing, particularly when your historic arch rival entered the ring approximately half as often as you did.

That Robinson refused to let La Motta duplicate his success is a testament to his focus and preparation. This is the "on any given Sunday" mindset that makes the

NFL business model so compelling. He fought La Motta the third time only twenty-one days after that isolated defeat. In between those two bouts he had time for a tune-up bout with Jackie Wilson a week before he decisioned La Motta.

Even the most focused athletes can become overconfident when they've beaten an opponent four times. This was their sixth bout, and this time more than pride and a winner's purse were at stake: They were fighting for the middleweight title that Jake La Motta now held after beating Marcel Cerdan of France.

On an evening of candlelight dinners and heart-shaped boxes of candy, La Motta—hairy-bellied, hairy-chested, and wearing black trunks—entered the ring like a Bronx garbage man. Robinson, in his usual slim white trunks and virtually hairless except for the trademark pompadour, looked like a model in comparison, though their weight difference was only four and one-half pounds. Even the black stripe on Robinson's shorts was narrower than La Motta's white. In their first meeting, the weight gap was somewhere between ten and sixteen pounds (depending on which side you believed); but even then, the difference in weight was far less important than the difference in conditioning and skill. Their rivalry was a study in contrasting styles. Robinson was a 17–5 favorite to win, but everybody knows those odds become irrelevant after the first punch is thrown.

Years later, at a fifty-something birthday party, Ray's cake was decorated with two boxing figures. Both had hair painted on their chests. Ray was adamant that neither represented him: His hair, he said, was always where it belonged—on his head. La Motta that night looked less like a Raging Bull than a Charging Buffalo as he descended the aisle and entered the ring.

La Motta's black shoes are taped over the laces, except for the last half-inch of leather going up the ankle to the calf. Robinson's have an inch of white sock showing above his white-laced black boots. The referee, Frank Sikora, wears a short-sleeved white shirt, no tie. He expects it to be a busy night. A scorecard dangles from his back pocket.

Robinson's people know that La Motta had trouble making weight and they set their strategy accordingly. In the early rounds, La Motta tries to connect with his powerful left hook. Robinson responds with jabs that bring him closer to the Raging Bull. The mind games have begun. Ray wants to show Jake that he has no fear of coming inside on the burly boxer. This strategy gives La Motta a lot of inside openings, but he never really connects. Robinson's tactics are revealed as a ploy and little more. He dances in, jabs, then stumbles back as La Motta charges. It all seems pointless until fatigue starts to show on La Motta's face. Coming into the fight underweight, La Motta lacks the energy reserves he's used to. Gradually, the Raging Bull becomes the lumbering bull. But neither fighter lands a decisive punch. The early rounds are called even by the judges.

In the middle of the scheduled fifteen-round fight, Robinson's game plan changes. Instead of teasing La Motta from inside, he begins to dance around him—vintage Sugar Ray—delivering hooks and dynamic combinations. La Motta tries to lure Robinson inside, but when he succeeds, the two men clinch: not just the boxer's rest, but like anacondas. When they break, it's with a flurry of combinations to each other's heads and bodies, each man targeting the other's vulnerable kidneys. In one clinch, La Motta tries to throw Robinson to the ground, wrestling style. The referee breaks them up. Robinson comes back with a series of stinging jabs. La Motta ignores them and keeps charging. Robinson's left is unremitting.

Here Ray reverts to an old tactic. He wants to keep jabbing, but if he stands still, La Motta charges inside, so Robinson skips backward, circling one way then another, firing punches as he goes. (Years later, Ali and Ray Leonard would master the same technique, and nonboxing aficionados would hail them as innovators; but Robinson did it long before, and he perfected it.) La Motta plods dully after him. Those in the know begin to suspect that the Bronx Bull never even experimented with the technique in the gym— had his sparring partner simulate Ray's patented backward attack—or tried to figure out a counter. Such preparation would have been a waste of time. La Motta was not a finesse boxer. To him, the odds were always 50–50: You hit the other guy or you missed; you won the bout or you lost. Strategy, beyond pushing forward, was not necessary.

As the fight progresses, Robinson abandons the jab in favor of lightning combinations: potential fight-ending punches coming from all directions and all angles. Flashbulbs begin to pop as photographers and reporters sense the end is near. Robinson ends one shower of shots on his toes, setting up for the next. The cheers get louder, more vicious.

Among the judges, curiously, the rounds are scored almost evenly—such is the power of a long-standing rivalry. La Motta apparently gets points for sheer guts: bulling in and blasting away like a tank while heavy artillery explodes around him.

The air is electric with anticipation as the bout enters its final rounds. In those days, fights could be a major test of stamina, scheduled for fifteen rounds instead of the modern twelve. Those last three rounds were dropped after the Larry Holmes-Randall "Tex" Cobb bloodbath in 1982, where statisticians determined that it was in those last three rounds, twelve through fifteen, that most injuries occurred. The carnage Holmes wrought on Cobb was so severe that Howard Cosell swore never to cover another professional bout.

In the eleventh round, Robinson pulls yet another trick out of his hat, again foreshadowing Ali. It is not a full-fledged rope-a-dope, but, backing into a neutral corner, Ray gives La Motta his head and permission to "wipe himself out" with a rain of fruitless blows against Robinson's gloves and forearms. Jake throws over two dozen punches—powerful combinations, a few landing on Robinson's smoothly muscular body—before observers lose count. And Robinson just stands there, covered up and taking it. When he perceives the bull to be weakening, he bounces off the ropes, pounding back. He stays on attack for the remainder of the fight.

The fighters move back to center ring. Ray hits Jake with a fairly low but legal left, followed by a relentless combination. La Motta keeps coming. Another Robinson flurry. One punch lands cleanly on the jaw. La Motta's head snaps back, but he doesn't go down. As the bell goes off, Robinson lands one more to the head.

The final round begins with the bull going to slaughter. Three Sugar Ray left hooks make contact. From one angle, Ray appears to be holding Jake with his left hand while hitting him with his right—using his head like a speed bag. It is a dance they have done before. Like two old lovers, they drift across the canvas. Robinson knows every blow will land, and La Motta knows he will never give up. Happy Valentine's Day.

In the end, for the first time, Jake tries for a clinch to gain relief. It doesn't work. The flurries keep coming, and La Motta has nowhere to go. He's been beaten to a bloody mess. The referee stops the fight. La Motta manages a grisly grin as he staggers toward his handlers. "You never put me down, Ray! You never put me down!" And he didn't. The line, heard only by the fighters, the referee, and those closest to them, was immortalized in the movie *Raging Bull*. It was what their rivalry was all about.

In an interview years later, La Motta said that if they hadn't stopped the fight, Robinson would have passed out from sheer exhaustion. The bout was called after Frank Sikora was given the signal by Dr. J. M. Houston of the Illinois State Athletic Commission. Boxing as a sport— let alone La Motta as an athlete—would hardly benefit from further gratuitous bloodshed. La Motta was in trouble, whether he admitted it or not.

For his part, Ray was finished with the fight, though he was far from falling down tired. He went to his corner with his arm initially raised by the referee; but then he threw them both up, realizing that he'd won and Jake was still standing. The look on his face was not so much jubilance as relief. Like any true rivalry, the fight could've gone either way. Winning five out of six bouts said something about Robinson that even La Motta's biggest boosters couldn't contest.

That night, La Motta refused help out of the ring, though Lord knows he could've used it. His face was pressed into an oxygen mask, a handler following with a portable green tank. It was forty minutes before they took it off. La Motta himself, predictably, remained unconvinced. "I fought Sugar Ray six times in all," he said, "and I should have won three of them, but . . . at any rate, as far as our careers are concerned, there's a curious relationship there. In one sense, he was the only guy I was never really able to nail the way I wanted to nail. *He was a nemesis to me.* But on the other hand, a lot of his reputation was built on the fact that he had beaten me. One fighter even said to me, 'Jake, I never figured Robinson was that good till after he'd fought you.'"

Even after retirement, La Motta remained competitive toward Robinson. "I mean he wasn't exactly a pansy," La Motta said, "and I think it still bugs him—I hope it still bugs him—that he was never able to flatten me. And I'm one of the few guys who ever took him." La Motta never admitted he had been hurt by Robinson. To Jake, "being hurt" meant being put on your back, and that never happened when he was in the ring with Ray. Robinson predicted that he would be the first to knock La Motta down, but never fulfilled that promise. For this, Robinson felt enormous respect for La Motta—one of the few boxers who could go the distance with him. He knew he hadn't broken the Raging Bull's spirit, and never would. Ray never forgot that first fight, the pain of a blow that brought tears to his battle-worn eyes, and the professional chagrin of being knocked from the ring. He wrote, "I had to share my joy [of winning that final bout] with

my respect for Jake. I got the decision, but I learned that
Jake La Motta was some animal."

Rivalries like Robinson-La Motta appeal to us because
they reduce sports complexities to their bare essentials.
They're pure. From a technical standpoint, the true beauty
of rivalry is that it allows direct comparison. We can watch
our hero mature against a continuous yardstick. Moreover,
the Robinson-La Motta fights were popular simply because
they were exciting bouts between great boxers that featured two antipodal styles of boxing.

Another reason this particular rivalry took on such vibrant life may have been that La Motta represented the
latest *White Hope*. Although Robinson was broadly ac-
cepted by white America, many fans still smarted from
the Jack Johnson era and they were uncomfortable when
a black man stayed on top for too long. This racial subtext
gave an extra edge to the Robinson-La Motta rivalry,
though it was usually below the surface and never touted
by the fighters themselves.

Modern promoters may be hesitant (at least publicly) to
play the race card, but that wasn't always so. The most
egregious examples of race-baiting in boxing came in the
July 4, 1910, bout between Jack Johnson and Jim Jeffries.
Johnson's previous bouts were never formally billed in
terms of race, but in this bout, the promoter, Tex Rickard,
sought permission from Jeffries and Johnson to paint the

contest in black and white. They agreed, and what could've been a clash of styles and talent formally became a two-man race war. La Motta writes in his autobiography that he did not realize he was a national figure until his first fight with Robinson; and the racial contrast it presented, especially in the approaching boil of the civil rights era, was clearly one of the reasons.

After that, the Great White Hope strategy too often became a substitute for true athletic rivalry. In 1982, there was really no technical reason to think that Gerry Cooney, a white fighter, posed a serious threat to Larry Holmes, the then-undefeated heavyweight champion. Although Cooney was a hulk of a man, his boxing skills were nothing extraordinary. Meanwhile, Holmes, who was super-sized as well, had skills of the highest order. Until the racial hype began, there wasn't anything especially compelling about the match.

With race as the undertone, each fighter was promised an amazing $10 million apiece. There was no reason for Cooney to be paid the same as the Champ, other than to make a mockery of "racial equality" and compensate him, perhaps, for getting publicly humiliated by a boxer who was out of his class. Sadly, legend has it that President Ronald Reagan had a phone line installed in Cooney's dressing room, not to Holmes's, for the traditional congratulatory call. Whether that says more about Reagan's shortcomings as a boxing analyst or as a president of *all* the people is unclear. The long life of the rumor alone tells us a great deal about the power of race, even near the end of the twentieth century.

Individual sports such as boxing and tennis are natural seedbeds for rivalry—racially motivated or not—and Sugar Ray had more than his share. Sugar Ray had at least half a dozen rivals who persistently popped in and out of his life, each vying for the limelight that he dominated. These rivalries captured the national imagination, and they did it without the help of HBO, ESPN, CNN, or Don King. Many of his early fights were not even filmed. His ring mates on the night of his farewell gala, Carmen Basilio, Randy Turpin, Carl "Bobo" Olson, and Gene Fullmer, had all spent a significant part of their careers hot on Robinson's trail.

The career of a successful boxer at that time was only as noteworthy as the rivalries that defined it. Sugar Ray Leonard's epic rematches with Roberto Duran and Thomas Hearns evoke the spirit of these serial competitions, as did Ali's perennial contests with Joe Frazier. Still, the number of opponents, the number of fights, and the number of years and weight classes that Robinson's career spanned put him far ahead of those who would come after him.

Boxing had always been fueled by such colorful contests. An ongoing rivalry somehow shapes the destiny of both fighters and captures the public's imagination. Without a strong rival to test one's mettle on the hero's journey, as Joseph Campbell put it, greatness is difficult to measure or achieve.

The boxing promoter Don King would fittingly become the king of rematches; he had a seemingly innate understanding of how best to seize the attention of the sporting public. He popularized the naming of fights. Without him we would've had no Rumble in the Jungle or Thrilla' in Manila. He was following Ali's lead of giving persistent rivals nicknames. Sonny Liston was the Big Ugly Bear, Floyd Patterson was the Rabbit, Earnie Shavers was the Acorn, and so on.

Much to the chagrin of Don King, savvy marketing was not always enough to stoke the flames of public passion. Rematches are sometimes scheduled, then cancelled, as quickly as a boxer can skip rope. When a new, more lucrative rival comes through the door, old rivalries can be tossed out the window. When Buster Douglas knocked out the seemingly invincible Mike Tyson on February 11, 1990 (Tyson was 37–0 with thirty-three knockouts) the world was shocked and cries for a rematch were heard before the final bell went quiet. Promoters, the media, and fans sharpened their knives for a big payday. However, Buster Douglas ate himself out of shape, sat on his laurels, and lost his title to the then-hungriest man in boxing, Evander Holyfield, before the schedules and profit-splitting details could be worked

out. Suddenly, nobody cared about a Tyson-Douglas rematch. Tyson-Holyfield was the only match that counted,
so that's what boxing delivered, along with several subse-
quent rematches. Buster Douglas watched as his celebrity
faded and, as anxious as he might have been to redeem
himself, or as satisfying as a knockout over Douglas might
have felt to Tyson, the public didn't share their sense of
rivalry; so a rematch never happened.

A true, career-long nemesis relationship is rare. Two
athletes may gain fame about the same time, offer contrasting styles and personalities—even racial differences—
and long profoundly to knock the guy out of the limelight;
but many things can happen to keep them apart: injuries,
scandals, manager or family intervention—anything.
When it happens, as it did with Robinson and La Motta,
especially in that final fight, it's a wonder to behold. The
professional turns personal and we all tune in, or buy tickets, to watch history being made.

The merger of the professional and the personal is what
makes a rivalry between individual athletes so much more
visceral than one between two teams. Ultimately, team rivalries are institutional, not personal. That's why Martina-
Chrissie, Connors-Borg, Nicklaus-Palmer, even Seabiscuit
and War Admiral matchups sell like cold beer in a humid
ballpark while big league teams often play to half-empty
stadiums. Personal rivalries strike a chord with people because that's the way we live our lives. We compete with

siblings for parental attention, classmates for scholarships, and coworkers for promotions. Our identification with one-on-one competition is clear. If you say Yankees-Red Sox, you still need to specify the year, the era, the pitchers, and the batters involved for the specific visual.

When Wilt played Russell, fans had to wait for the right game. Schedule rotation and dates locked far in advance dictate rivalries in team sports far more than the ambitions and talents of individual athletes. We can still debate which football, hockey, baseball, or basketball star is better in a given position, but we can never isolate their strengths and weaknesses in an individual, head-to-head comparison because too many other players just get in the way. Boxing matches, on the other hand, are scheduled almost on the fly. They are dictated by public pressure, a boxer's health, and the whiff of profit, or greatness, that surrounds a specific pairing.

In boxing, all you need is two names. One such pairing was between Robinson and Randy Turpin. Robinson lost to Turpin on July 10, 1951, in London. This was a huge upset by the champion of the British Isles. While in Paris, and leading up to the Turpin bout, Robinson was not training properly. "There were no workouts," according to Gordon Parks, who covered this European tour as a photographer. "Sugar Ray played at golf through the days, and at card tables late into the nights. Turpin, a dockside-type brawler, trained like a man possessed."

In London, after losing the bout, the American war-
rior embraced his British counterpart at center ring. Robinson looked dazed, not from blows but as if he had been
mugged by reality. He could not believe it had happened.
He looked like a parody of himself. He was drenched in
sweat, and the process chemicals reacted to make his hair
essentially stand on end as though it were smeared with
butch wax. That famous Robinson image of cool—of col-
lected self-assurance—had changed dramatically into
one of defeat and disbelief.

At Leamington Spa, the atmosphere welcoming Turpin
home resembled a VE-Day celebration. Turpin, looking
out of his element as champ, was led to huge microphones
in front of the crowd. He pulled out a sheet of paper and
awkwardly began to read a speech: "It was a great fight on
Tuesday and I'm naturally very proud to bring the middleweight crown back to England."

As Turpin began to squirm, the audience began to
cheer. They didn't want to hear "prepared remarks," they
wanted to hear what was in his heart. Bordering him were
several very British-looking men with medallions around
their necks. He continued to read awkwardly from his
notes.

"Well," he said finally, placing his hands shyly over his
face, "well, I'm not much at making speeches. But anyway you all know what I mean." The crowd loved it. He
staged an upset victory and brought the title to England.

He was the hero of the day—Sugar Ray's nemesis. He didn't have to say anything else.

Across the Atlantic, Robinson returned to a roaring crowd at New York's City Hall. Mayor Impellitteri introduced him, foreshadowing that farewell evening still more than a decade away. Robinson spoke from his heart on this occasion as well. "I promise you that on September 12th I'll do my sincere utmost to again bring the middleweight championship back to America."

Robinson's City Hall speech epitomized the Sugar Ray cool. He and his companions wore light-colored suits and ties. The ex-Champ still looked like a champ. He announced that he had had "a very nice time in Europe." Those words really said it all. Critics had complained that the former Champ spent too much time partying in Paris before the fight, that he had not trained adequately. More informed Robinson-watchers knew better. There was something about Turpin's technique that was destined to give Sugar Ray trouble.

Robinson knew that he had let down not only himself but also his fans and America, and he said so. The return bout was set for two months after the London defeat. The promoters didn't waste much time, but their big problem was holding the fighters back. Turpin wanted to show that his win was no fluke and Robinson needed to show that it was.

Turpin came to America filled with confidence. Preparing to leave London, he told his fans, "Well, I'm on my way at last, and I will not let the British people down. I'm going to win." He wore a black beret and traveled in a Rolls Royce. This champ wanted to look like a champ. The "British Sugar Ray" had women hanging on to the big car's running board. He even journeyed from Southampton, England, to New York City in high style aboard the *Queen Mary*.

Turpin's father was a soldier from British Guyana and his mother was English. But there was no Tiger Woods–type multicultural marketing opportunity. He was simply the "British Negro." Back then one drop of Negro blood determined your racial fate, there was no fudging on blackness. Their bout at the Polo Grounds was sold out. More than sixty-one thousand showed up for the fight, and this when the live gate was still the key to making money in the fight game.

This night was special in another way. Interest in Robinson was so high that promoters experimented with closed circuit television: live action piped into movie theaters and shown on small screens, strategically placed. This was an innovative revenue source that would last until the advent of cable television and pay-per-view— the equivalent of selling thousands of tickets at ringside. The fight was shown at fourteen theaters in eleven cities across the United States. Thirty-five thousand fans outside of the Polo Grounds were able to watch it as if they were there.

It was that vicarious "You Are There" quality of live television that gave video technology its early boost. The three thousand fans at the Warner Brothers Stanley Theater in Philadelphia drank orange juice and ate popcorn as if they were killing time in the cheap seats in a real arena, waiting for a real-life bout to start. When the "Star Spangled Banner" and "God Save the King" played over the theater speakers, the crowd instinctively stood up, put their hands over their hearts, and saluted the grainy screen.

The bout gets underway with a flourish. "Work on him!" the ringside audience shouts. Robinson again wears white trunks. Turpin is much more mobile than most of the opponents Robinson has faced. That unaccustomed mobility immediately gives Robinson trouble.

Turpin bobs up and down, weaves back and forth, but he lacks Ray's lateral movement. One punch, then another, pops out of the jack-in-the-box and lands on the challenger. Turpin's style is unorthodox and Ray keeps his distance, keeping in motion, figuring things out. This time Robinson is better prepared—no doubt about it—both physically and mentally. There had been no late nights in Paris or shoddy accommodations this time around.

This battle looks more and more like a traditional Robinson fight. Throughout the middle rounds, Ray gathers momentum: jabbing, connecting with a series of lightning combinations, some delivered while retreating. Always he keeps moving, dancing rings, literally, around his opponent.

In the tenth round, Robinson goes in for the kill. He moves quickly, but perhaps not wisely. Turpin head-butts, opening a gash over Ray's right eye. Robinson sees his own blood. Fire fills his gloves and he hits Turpin with a solid right. Robinson's reaction is typical of many boxers, at least the ones with heart. If they see their blood, they know the referee does, too. If they don't act fast, the officials might call the fight. The entire right side of Robinson's face is red.

Turpin now targets his opponent's weakness. If he can score just a few more hits on the bloody gash, he can win on a TKO. The jack-in-the-box pops up, once, twice. A right-cross from Robinson. Turpin goes down, flat on his back. It is 2:52 in the tenth. Flashbulbs pop.

Turpin climbs to one knee for the mandatory eight count. As he gets up, Robinson charges in, driving him to the ropes. It's all Turpin can do to catch a few of the punches on his arms and gloves. Counterpunching is out of the question. He has nothing left. Robinson's attack is continuous, brutal, merciless. Finally, after multiple blows to Turpin's head, the referee steps in and pushes Robinson away. He inspects Turpin's eyes then hugs him, telling him it's over. New York police immediately surround the ring. The Turpin curse had been lifted. Sugar Ray kept his promise.

As with many boxing victories that come without a knock-out or a clear decision, the loser was in disbelief. "That referee should not have stopped the bout." Turpin said in interviews after the fight. "My head was clear and my body did not feel weak." According to Turpin, the ring's doctor agreed. "When the doctor interviewed me in the ring about a minute after the fight, he found me in good shape. I remember when he asked me what date it was. I replied: 'It was the twelfth but now it's the thirteenth' because it was just after midnight. The doctor himself admitted that the fight should never have been stopped."

Theatergoers had paid $2.60 at the door to see America regain the middleweight title. This included the 90-cent price of a movie. In Philadelphia, they filed out once the fight was over. In Chicago, brawls broke out in theaters and out on the street. Unlike in Philadelphia, tickets weren't sold in advance. As a result, many fans were turned away, and this upset lots of Robinson's followers. They stormed the doors at the State Lake Theatre in the Loop, Uptown, Broadway, and on Lawrence and Tivoli.

With a gate of $768,000, and $200,000 for movie rights (newsreels, not a dramatization), as well as $50,000 for the closed-circuit television, this was the first $1 million non-heavyweight fight in history.

Turpin had held the title for just sixty-four days. Robinson never backed away from a serious contender, although while at the championship level he chose his battles wisely. The ebb and flow of title takings and title losings were mind-boggling compared to the slow pace of arranging title bouts in any division today. Consider the following: When Robinson finally won that middleweight title from La Motta in 1951, he lost it five months later in the first bout with Turpin. Twenty-five rounds and two months later, he won that title back. Turpin spoiled for a rematch, but Sugar Ray had nothing left to prove. This was one of those wise moves. Another bout with Turpin could have gone the wrong way for him. In 1952, he defended the title against Bobo Olson and Rocky Graziano. He then went after the light heavyweight title held by Joey Maxim.

After a twenty-two-month retirement, Ray came back; and after six fights, he won back the middleweight crown, this time from Bobo Olson in Chicago in 1955. More than gaining a title, he gained some fans with that victory. He displayed emotion unseen before breaking down on the way to the locker room. He'd been counted out by so many, but he had regained the title. Even with that, this level of emotion was unexpected from the man whose reputation for arrogance, coolness, and a lack of patriotism was legendary. But the loss to Maxim had brought him down a few pegs. This showing of emotion served to humanize him. And this was just the beginning of a cycle of weaving rivalries that would make his career unparalleled. Ray's ability to come back after a defeat was on display time and time again in the 1950s, but, like all of us, he was not getting any younger.

After giving Olson the chance to win the middleweight title back in 1956, he fought Gene Fullmer next, who took the title from Ray on January 2, 1957, in a fifteen-round decision. But Robinson regained the title from Fullmer four months later. He was thirty-five years old. Then Robinson lost the title in a fifteen-rounder with Carmen Basilio in New York in 1957; then he won it back again, from Basilio in a fifteen-round decision in Chicago in 1958. Robinson lost the title, for the last time, to Paul Pender in Boston on January 22, 1960. On June 10 of that same year, he lost a fifteen-round title decision to Paul Pender, in Boston again. Fullmer put the middleweight title he held on the line and fought Ray to a draw on December 3, 1960. On March 4, 1961, the old rivals met again in a final fight in Las Vegas.

Sugar Ray lost that bout to Fullmer and never regained the title again. But the decade of rivals in the 1950s and, before that, the rivalry with La Motta in the 1940s—those competitions, the high volume, the longevity, and the multiple opponents, are without comparison in sport.

Larry Holmes, Mike Tyson, Roger Federer, and Shaquille O'Neal: None of these great winners had or has rivalries comparable to Sugar Ray's. Michael Jordan may

be the only athlete to reach legendary heights without a
clearly designated rival. He arrived on the heels of Magic
and Bird, and was basically out of the game when less
dominant players—at least when it came to star power,
such as Shaquille O'Neal and Allen Iverson—began to
exert their celebrity.

On a personal level, we all wish secretly that we could
one day "get even" with a longtime nemesis, no matter
the field of endeavor: from the schoolyard bully who stole
our lunch to an unappreciative boss who, psychologically
anyway, "decks" us every day. Life obliges us to meet these
challengers regularly. When we lose, it hurts. When we
win, it feels great, but we know that our nemesis, or a different rival, will soon reappear. After a while, we begin to
realize that it is the battle, not the victory, that counts.
Rivalries are about perseverance and character; they
come back for more even after we suffer a bloodied nose.

Robinson's career was defined by rivalry. The mutual
respect and public admiration that engendered was one
of the qualities that set him above his contemporaries.
The ring on that famous farewell night was full of Robinson's rivals.

Although we love to see Tiger Woods play—if for no
other reason than to enjoy his artistry in golf—we'd love it
even more if he had a nemesis dogging his footsteps, just as
Arnold Palmer battled Jack Nicklaus, or Martina Navratilova battled Chris Evert. Even horse-race handicappers

hate a predictable winner because the odds just don't pay off. We prefer an outcome that's in doubt. Sometimes, fate steps in and provides some drama. Muhammad Ali was supposed to clean Ken Norton's clock. When Norton broke Ali's jaw, a rivalry was created.

In a very real sense, celebrity-athletes know they are perceived to be only as good as the best opponents fate sends against them. As true competition wanes, so does the star of our best athletes. Larry Holmes learned this the hard way. He wanted to pursue Rocky Marciano's record as an undefeated heavyweight world champion, but he was burdened by the lack of big-name rivals. One evening, after an easy victory over a long-shot contender, Holmes said, "Rocky Marciano couldn't hold my jock strap." That was frustration talking, not a champion for the ages. Rocky, by that time, had become a national icon. A true sports celebrity. Holmes was still looking for his place in sports history.

For us regular folks, all this can be inspiring. If my favorite sports celebrity can meet the challenge of arch rivalry, maybe I can, too. If he rises to that challenge consistently, win or lose, he deserves my respect—and that's what most of us want out of life.

PART THREE

OBLIGATIONS

Sugar Ray tending bar in Harlem, June 25, 1953. Photo: Corbis.

DEDICATIONS

CHAPTER SIX

OVERREACHING

He was quite a terrible singer.

—WOODY ALLEN ON SUGAR RAY

"I am here to meet with Mr. Weintraub."

Ray wore a dark two-button suit, black tie knotted perfectly, public smile on display. He was responding to a reporter who had shouted, "What are you doing in Los Angeles?"

It was a relatively cold day for LA. The propellers churning the air over the tarmac at LAX added velocity to the spring winds. Robinson stood at the base of the TWA stairs. There was no concourse in 1959, just a roll-up stairway that met the airplane. With or without fanfare, the press corps had been alerted.

Ray was at a point in his career where no one was sure what he would do next. Conjecture about the next dark-horse contender had turned to speculation that Ray was going to make a rare leap into the heavyweight division.

Ray and his camp didn't deny the possibility that a bout with Floyd Patterson—currently heavyweight champion of the world—was on the horizon. The jump from welterweight to middleweight, 147 to 160 pounds, was less than the leap from welterweight to heavyweight, where the big boys only started at 175 pounds.

Before Robinson's initial retirement in 1952, some urged him to fight the only undefeated heavyweight champion in history, Rocky Marciano. Ray had just become a middleweight, defeating La Motta despite a weight disadvantage of more than fifteen pounds. It would have been a stretch to go after a heavyweight, especially one of Marciano's stature. This feat had been tried before by other fighters, without success. There was also talk of Robinson's fighting the light heavyweight Archie Moore, but Ray wasn't interested. It seemed that the money was never right. Rumors about a Robinson-Patterson bout, however, began to circulate now that Ray seemed immune to the natural laws that governed other boxers; a $1 million guarantee was being offered by Sy Weintraub, the Hollywood producer and the one-time owner of Panavision, to get him to fight the current heavyweight champ. When those kind of numbers—and a name like Sugar Ray's—were bandied about, people had to pay attention.

Some compared Robinson's dilemma to the choice made by a smaller middleweight, Stanley Ketchel, to fight Jack Johnson in the early 1900s. At the press conference announcing their October 16, 1909, bout, Johnson appeared in his usual sartorial splendor: a three-button pinstriped suit, starched shirt, and glossy "Stacy Adams" shoes; Ketchel wore an oversized overcoat, obviously padded and buttoned to the neck, along with a pair of high-heeled cowboy boots. Unaided by such special effects, the six-foot-tall Johnson weighed in at 209 pounds to Ketchel's five foot nine and 160 pounds.

Though it might have been billed the "mismatch of the century," Ketchel actually did gain a knockdown early in the fight. Furious, Johnson came back with a single crushing blow and relieved Ketchel of several teeth. The bout went downhill after that, and Johnson won handily.

Robinson, unlike Ketchel, had reason to think he just might beat a bona fide heavyweight. Patterson wanted nothing to do with this bout. Apart from having everything to lose, he was a reluctant celebrity who seemed uncomfortable with his fame. All the heavyweight champion of the world would gain by beating a middleweight was more unwanted attention. And if he really hurt Robinson—a popular crossover athlete—he might well be demonized for "picking on" a smaller legendary fighter. It is possible that Patterson's handlers pointed out that Robinson was no ordinary fighter, that beating him wouldn't be easy, and that if Patterson agreed to the bout, he would be vaulted to even higher celebrity. But such logic would have fallen on deaf ears because Patterson did not desire fame and did not let such considerations make his professional decisions.

As it turned out, any reluctance on Patterson's part didn't matter. On June 26, 1959, Patterson lost his title to Ingemar Johansson in the fifth round of a bout in Yankee Stadium. That put a stop to Weintraub's negotiations with Robinson. Aside from focusing on Patterson's rematch with Johansson, Weintraub remained occupied with Hollywood productions focused on tales of Tarzan and Sherlock Holmes. In a way, it was just as well. Many people considered the Robinson-Patterson match a gimmick at best. A heavyweight rematch was what the public craved. But until that upset, Robinson actively pursued the Patterson project: "After all," he said, "you don't laugh at a million dollars."

Robinson's almost pursuit of the heavyweight championship, after making his name in the welter- and middleweight ranks, exemplifies a dilemma always faced by the all-time greats: Where do you go after you've reached the top of the heap? The greatest always want to do more. Michael Jordan tried baseball. Some, like Jim Brown and Merlin Olsen, go into show business—on stage, on television, or in films: a natural transition since the best have always understood that pro sports have always been a form of entertainment. Many become broadcasters now that the venue for telegenic commentators has exploded on cable and satellite television. Some open restaurants or car dealerships; others tout products. Product endorsements in our consumer culture can provide a good living after a superstar hangs up the gloves, the cleats, or the nine iron. George Foreman has probably been the most successful in linking his name to a specific product: the George Foreman Grill.

Robinson had already tried boxing above his weight division in a light heavyweight championship bout with Joey Maxim (born Giuseppe Antonio Berardinelli) on June 25, 1952. Robinson's goal at the time was to win titles in three weight classes, and only two boxers had done this before. "The people wanted to see me fight the light heavyweight champion," Robinson proclaimed in a documentary years later, but with Robinson you had to know there was personal drive involved in the decision as well.

The signing for the Maxim-Robinson fight was a minidrama on its own. Although today there are still events announcing bouts, the formal signing is often private. Joey Maxim appeared in a light blazer, open-collared dark shirt, and shiny cuff links; his jet black hair was heavily oiled. Robinson wore a long-sleeved light sweater with the collar of a light blue shirt sticking out. Unlike Ketchel of an earlier generation, he made no effort to look bigger or heavier than he was. Robinson had supreme confidence

in his abilities as he headed into the bout that night of
June 25, 1952.

The subway ride to the stadium was unbearable, and
the ringside temperature soared higher than 104 degrees,
the hottest temperature recorded on that date in New
York history. The outdoor fight had been delayed two days
because of rain. The drops had departed, but the moisture
was still in the air. Ray's wife at the time, Edna Mae, described the atmosphere as that of a "Turkish bath."

Robinson wore black trunks this time instead of his
usual white. A bad omen. Goldstein, the referee, showed
up in a long-sleeved shirt, the only one in the arena.
Coats and ties, the usual garb for a title fight, were shed
faster than saddles after a horse race.

The first round starts with Robinson attacking in his traditional style. Both fighters are drenched in sweat from
the beginning. His fast combinations back Maxim up and
put the champ on the defensive. Fans see immediately
that Maxim's greater size, once touted as the potential de-
ciding factor by boxing pundits, has no impact on Robinson: He is the better boxer.

In round two, Robinson staggers Maxim with another
combination. Maxim comes back with a flurry of punches.
By the third round, both boxers look like cooked noodles.
Robinson offers an easy head shot to Maxim. It was probably a fake—an attempt to get Maxim to expend more

energy—but the big man didn't go for it. The name
Maxim was given to him because his punches had reminded a commentator of a similarly named machine
gun. It proved a misnomer on this night. Maxim is obviously trying to conserve his energy in the sweltering heat.

The bell sounds and Robinson goes to a neutral corner.
One of his cornermen comes over, grabs him, and leads
him by a slippery arm back to his corner. Ray collapses on
his stool.

At the end of the early rounds, Robinson is clearly
ahead on points. He is fighting from a crouch, though,
which is unusual for Ray because it's the hallmark of plod-
ding sluggers; but he continues to move from this stance.
In retrospect, observers realized it was the only way he
could protect himself from a significantly heavier opponent with a longer reach. When he struck out—with jabs
or a combination—it was like the blowfish who expands
at the last second, surprising would-be predators. Today,
though, the bigger fish aren't biting.

The fight continues. Maxim absorbs a lot of punishment while he preserves his energy. He throws very few
punches and leans on Robinson whenever possible. He is
fighting a very smart fight, especially in that record heat.
Robinson's body is drenched with sweat; his hair glistens
like a mop. Still, other than his stance, there is nothing
to make anyone think this won't be a typical Robinson
victory. As the boxers crouch, amble, and drip their way

around the ring, the crowd tries to cool itself with paper fans. Humidity shellacs their shirts and blouses to their bodies like poorly hung wallpaper. The beer and soft-drink vendors are willing to sacrifice the night's tips if the fight will only end.

In the tenth round, referee Goldstein gasps like a goldfish taken from his bowl. He takes some smelling salts between rounds, but that is of little help. Next to Robinson, he had been the most active man in the ring. The ringside doctor, Alexander Schiff, takes a look at Goldstein between rounds, but he tells Schiff, "I'm O.K." Shortly after the tenth begins, he staggers into the ropes. The doc jumps into the ring and tells Goldstein that the fight is over for him.

A new referee, Ray Miller, a younger man, comes in to finish the fight. Later in life, Robinson would show film of this bout to friends and joke about how the fight went on so long: "The referee grew more hair."

In the eleventh, with a new referee in charge, Robinson looks stellar. Maxim is holding his own, but Robinson is way ahead on points. In the twelfth, however, things change. Ray staggers around the ring like a Harlem wino. Maxim, unperturbed, continues to play his own game. After all, he is a boxer who trained in New Orleans. He knows about heat and humidity.

In the thirteenth, Robinson looks shriveled. He's gasping for air. He keeps after Maxim, confident—like virtually everyone else at the bout—that he is ahead on points.

Robinson whiffs a punch and goes down. Maxim stalks closer, but shows no intention of going in for the kill. Robinson gets up and stumbles to his corner. Maxim doesn't even follow. Unlike Graziano, Maxim understands how dangerous injured prey can be. Robinson is wilting. A smart fighter would just let him punch himself out.

The bell clangs, ending the round, just as Robinson lurches out and lands a right cross to Maxim's chin. Maxim shrugs it off.

The bell for the fourteenth sounds. The cornermen use ice and smelling salts on Robinson, but he doesn't respond. The ring doctor steps up and makes his assessment. "Can you go on?" Schiff asks. Robinson nods yes, but the doctor shakes his head. The fight is called in Maxim's favor. He retains the light-heavyweight championship of the world by virtue of forethought.

This defeat tipped the scales in Ray's decision to retire. He blamed it on a gradual deterioration of his skills. Sugar Ray had always prided himself on being smarter than any boxer around. But he misjudged Maxim. As the columnist Arthur Dailey put it, "Robinson, a smart fighter, didn't fight a smart fight."

Robinson was clear in explaining to the *New York Times* why he was finished:

I do not feel I can any longer give the public my best as it has come to recognize it, and I know better than anyone else how good I am and what my limitations are. I find I can't move in the ring with the same speed, dispatch and accuracy. My instinct used to guide my hands and feet. I could see the opening in a flash and, in the same twinkle, handle the situation. Now the co-ordination isn't there any more. No one knows that better than I do.

Apparently, Robinson was much closer to death on that hot, humid evening than most people realized. He refused hospitalization and was taken home by his wife. There he lay in bed while his body withered from dehydration and blistered with heat sores. Intravenous fluids would have helped, but tap water and juice taken by mouth were all he got; even those were tough to get down. The first swallows were thrown up. Edna Mae's clothes were ruined, and the housekeeper had to change the sheets.

Reflecting on that night and the explanation given by Robinson, Maxim told reporters years later that he never understood why people blamed Robinson's loss on the heat. He asked rhetorically, "Did I have air conditioning in my corner? I pushed him all night. He knocked himself out."

Robinson's attempt to win a title so far beyond his original weight class would foreshadow the actions of those greats to come after him. This sort of overreaching would seem to be an occupational hazard of our greatest athletes.

In the mid-1990s Michael Jordan was living one of many dreams as a member of the NBA-champion Chicago Bulls, but he decided to pursue a baseball career. The key to this second dream was provided by the man for whom he had won the NBA world championship, Jerry Reinsdorf. Through Reinsdorf, Jordan had joined the double-A team in the White Sox organization. Reinsdorf, who owned the Chicago White Sox and the Chicago Bulls, fulfilled this particular fantasy.

The Class AA Birmingham Barons made their home at Hoover Metropolitan Stadium in Alabama, and it was not universally popular, particularly among baseball aficionados, that Jordan had joined their ranks. By every account (other than Jordan's search for personal satisfaction), baseball just wasn't in his future. He had spent his adult life in basketball. He had sacrificed whatever baseball skills he had possessed as a child to develop a different set of reflexes and a different way of thinking. While pursuing this (perhaps unrealistic) dream, he batted .202 and had three home runs. Minor league pitchers struck him out 30 percent of the time. That's not greatness; it's dilettantism.

Leaving sports altogether is one option when a celebrity feels it's the end of the line. Here's what some people saw one night on the popular *Ed Sullivan Show:* The rope skips at warp speed. *Whoosh-tap*. *Whoosh-tap*. A stiff and tight four-in-hand necktied figure walks on stage, and after

the brief pause, Sullivan says, lips pursed, looking sky-
ward, "The new middleweight champion of the world—
Sugar Ray Robinson!" He extends his hand to the rope
skipping figure.

This was the nature of Sugar Ray's transition to show-
biz dancer and singer. It was not Ray's talent as a dancer
that enabled him to go on tour in 1953 and 1954—his fall-
back plan after the Joey Maxim defeat—it was his stage
presence and desire to please a crowd that carried the day.
Ray always said that each fight was a kind of show, a man-
date to please the crowd, an obligation to give his best.
This desire was part PR, part professional pride, but it was
also a heartfelt plea for approval. Since then, a number of
athletes have followed in his tracks and subjected themselves to the vagaries of a fickle, half-drunk cabaret crowd,
but few have matched Ray's sense of presence, and that
made all the difference.

An article of the period, titled "Sugar Ray's New Face,"
reported that Robinson even underwent plastic surgery to
boost this new, postretirement career. It said he had un-
dergone surgery to "remove scar tissue from beneath the
eyes and bob his nose" and that "it was a definite cue his
fighting days were over."

One of the first pro athletes to turn entertainer was
Jack Johnson. He went through various incarnations, including Vaudevillian and even Shakespearian. In one
phase, while Johnson was touring Europe, his stage show

included lifting weights, breaking chains, and hoisting a group of men while his wife sang a song. He even went on to bullfighting—without much success—but at least he escaped these experiments in Spain and Mexico with his anatomy intact.

NBA stars Shaquille O'Neal and Allen Iverson joined this exclusive club as rappers. Their musical output did not necessarily leave their world a better place. Ron Artest is testing that field, too. Successful athletes of the past had a more dignified exit from the sports arena and, because of the greater emphasis on talent rather than hype in those days, a better track record at the ticket booth or box office.

Chuck Connors originally played for the Yankees, then parlayed his stalled career into a successful television series, *The Rifleman*. Jim Brown left the NFL in the 1960s at the height of his career to star in movies, including *The Dirty Dozen* and *100 Rifles*. Upon his retirement from the NFL, Merlin Olsen became a fixture on television, notably in *Little House on the Prairie* and FTD flower commercials. Jackie Robinson as well as Joe Louis (and numerous other athletes) starred in biopics based on their life stories. The last thirty-game winner in baseball, Denny McClain, played the Hammond B3 on the *Ed Sullivan Show*, and Joe Frazier had limited success with a singing group called *The Knockouts*. Even before Robinson, athletes such as Red Grange and Johnny Weissmuller went from the gym to the film studio without breaking a sweat. Then again, making the difficult, or the near impossible, look easy has always been the calling card of our athletic heroes.

Robinson earned an unprecedented $10,000 per week in his debut as a dancer, more than Fred Astaire and Gene Kelly commanded throughout the 1950s. Sugar Ray danced in Las Vegas, Paris, and New York, though his charm and popularity carried him further than fancy foot-work. In France, he added rope-jumping to his act because his audience expected it. He received mixed reviews. The mainstream media praised him for his natural charm but cast a jaundiced eye on his hoofing. *Time* magazine, for one, called Sugar a "second-rate song and dance man."

Notwithstanding all this, Robinson enjoyed his new lifestyle. Dancing took a lot of tedious practice, but so did training for a fight; and his nights were free and not sub-jected to self-imposed curfews and diet regimens. More-over, Robinson was now able to show off his wardrobe. In his debut, he changed costumes six times. If financial prob-lems arose, he knew he could always return to the ring. Boxing paid more than cabaret, and although he felt he had talent as a dancer, he knew his earning potential was limited. As the novelty wore off, so did the huge paydays.

"Not enough money?" Ray must have asked his ac-countant with an incredulous look. "How could that be? Everything is in order. We need to double check that." But no amount of checking was going to clear the mountain of debt he had accumulated while he had been on the road: living the high life, partying, and entertaining. Through a combination of neglect, mismanagement, theft, and lawsuits, Sugar Ray was in deep financial trouble. Robinson's businesses and lavish lifestyle had been in danger before his retirement in December 1952 even began. The only way to solve it was to get back into the ring.

His first fight after retirement was on November 29, 1954: an exhibition in Hamilton, Ontario, against his friend and training partner, Gene Burton. The first non-exhibition bout was against Joe Rindone in Detroit, in which Robinson won in a sixth-round knockout. Ray then came up against Ralph "Tiger" Jones. This was the true comeback bout: his first credible opponent after getting off of the stage. Robinson lost.

Battling with Jones Ray was never really *in trouble* in the technical sense, but he knew that he was losing. Throughout the fight he kept watching his corner and the timekeeper. His main objective didn't seem to be beating the other guy, but hanging in there until the round was over. He knew what it took to win a fight, and in that fight he did not have it in him, at least not at that particular moment. It was as though the famous Sugar Ray heart had been mortgaged to the bank. He felt ashamed. "I know one thing," Ray said after that loss to Jones, "I'm not through, and I'll fight again."

Following Robinson's loss, his cornermen, George Gainford and Harry Wiley, were so disappointed by the performance of their hero that they quit. Eventually, though, the two of them, along with the rest of his entourage, did come back. Even though many of the faces were the same, this second time around it is fair to say that Robinson had two boxing careers.

The first ended with the Maxim fight. It was in this era, too, that he began his public resurrection. Until he had established a new persona, the military problem, the aura of arrogance, the fancy clothes, and the fancier car all worked against him. There was more than a little racism among his critics, too: Those whites *and* blacks who thought he had upset the apple cart without just cause viewed him as too *uppity*.

His comeback wiped some of the slate clean. But perseverance in this second career phase enabled him to convert many of those fans and almost-fans who had deserted him. The Robinson story became one of determination. Sugar Ray was not alone in making comebacks, and the urge (or need) to do so is not unique to athletes. "This is something I never thought could possibly happen," Phil Jackson told a packed press conference in June 2005 in Los Angeles. After a year away from the NBA, with nine championships in hand, he re-upped for three more years to coach a team with whom all observers thought he had irreconcilable differences.

The team had fallen on hard times and Jackson missed the locker room, so an unlikely comeback deal was signed. Coaches, politicians, actors, pop singers—and most famously, athletes—love to return to the art that defined their lives. Sometimes, like Robinson, they do it because they have no choice.

The world watched with excitement and nostalgia as Muhammad Ali and Sugar Ray Leonard both made final ill-fated comebacks, long after the mold had been set by Sugar Ray. In team sports, the comeback is less common.

George Foreman threatened to reenter the ring yet again at the age of fifty-five. Usually, these "triumphal returns" are mere sideshows, sad attempts at hanging on, just as a famous Shakespearean actor past his prime might take bit parts in horror movies just to make ends meet or to see his name one last time on a theater marquee. Aging athletes seldom deliver the magic that made them famous, and they're foolish even to try. Ali could not; neither could Sugar Ray Leonard. Although Ray Robinson and Joe Louis had legitimate excuses to return to the ring—and at least a fighting chance, age wise, to do so with dignity before failing flesh gave out—today's top athletes do not. Today, most athletic superstars have made millions from their sport. If they go back into the arena, it's less often than in the past to support their families.

Robinson earned $4 million over the span of his boxing career. That's what an NBA first-round draft pick may expect straight out of high school for his first three years alone. The minimum for an NBA veteran is more than $1 million on top of that. Many receive more as a signing bonus than Sugar Ray received in a lifetime. In short, Sugar Ray was forced to extend his career because he signed checks his retirement couldn't cash.

One thing that differentiates sports superstars, *champs*, from the rest of life's success stories is longevity. You rarely get too old to be a physician before the traditional societal retirement age. You don't have to set aside your mechanic's grease gun or machinist's punch press because you have turned thirty-five. The unique thing about coming back to a sport you love and do well is the siren's call that attracted you to it in the first place. At some point you discovered you had a gift, and a few farsighted people helped you realize it. Following that dream brought you fame and fortune and self-esteem. Adulation, heroism, and the luxury of cultivating personal style, and being well rewarded for it, are powerful narcotics.

Athletes who overextend themselves and try to be stars in too many venues are destined for failure. We encourage them to set the bar too high, then chastise them when they fail to jump it. The modern list of successful two-sport athletes is brief. It pretty much ends after Deion Sanders and Bo Jackson. Jim Thorpe, the legendary star of track and field, baseball and football, may come to mind, but only because he stands alone in such a barren field.

For that matter, how many people, outside of sports, have been successful at more than one job? How many CEOs go from one industry to another with an unbroken string of success? How many quit business altogether to become astronauts, or how many astronauts leave NASA to become rock stars? Certainly, there are those who succeed in serial careers, some careers (such as football and boxing) are the gift of youth, but others—politics and teaching, for example—reward maturity. Unfortunately, many athletes, like Peter Pan, think that they will never have to grow up, that they will succeed at whatever they choose to do, no matter how unrealistic the goal.

Athletic celebrity makes a wonderful passport and can open many doors, but it doesn't suspend the laws of nature. Sugar Ray sought to extend himself as far as he could, and fans supported him—as long as they had reason to. Then Ray, and his fans, had to return to reality.

CHAPTER SEVEN

ENTOURAGE

"We just couldn't leave anybody, so we all came," Robinson's trainer, George Gainford, told *Time* magazine. As the baggage was unloaded in France, Sugar Ray heard stewards saying to each other that this was "the boxer and his *entourage*." Workers kept asking where all this stuff belonged, and the distinctive word *entourage* jumped out. It belonged to Sugar Ray's party: his colleagues and traveling companions. Sugar Ray used the word to describe his traveling party from that day forward.

Time depicted the scene as follows: "A corps of panting bellboys wrestled with 32 trunks and 15 suitcases, containing (among other items) three radio sets, 140 jazz records, six punching bags, ten pairs of boxing gloves." The cast generally consisted of fourteen people: Robinson's manager, his trainer, a masseuse, a barber, a golf instructor, and various gofers and other anticipated boxing staff. The entourage was soon joined by Jimmy Karoubi, a four-foot-four dwarf hired as a "bodyguard" and interpreter. Karoubi reportedly spoke five languages. It was with Karoubi's help that Robinson would deliver a phrase in French here and there following his half dozen trips throughout Europe.

Absent cell phones, messages during the tours of Europe were relayed publicly to Robinson. Sometimes the press would record George Gainford reporting, sheltering the mouthpiece of the phone and announcing the impressive "Robinson, it's the American Ambassador."

A modern day news helicopter would have focused in on the sea of luggage leading the Robinson entourage onto the cruise ship *Le Liberté* at the front end of the trip. The New York–based porters struggled with leather stacked high on steel carts. Most of the luggage had shiny brass corners and plush leather handles, and it smelled fresh and newly purchased. Leather luggage was nothing extraordinary in the mid-twentieth-century. Wicker suitcases and heavy satchels were the other options. But this was a lot of luggage by any standard. Most of the baggage that wasn't new had hauled boxing equipment to matches and camps throughout Sugar Ray's career and showed the wear and tear that was still absent from the Champ's face and body.

As they set off, the attire of Robinson and his traveling companions was lightweight business suits and ties. The garb was all loose-fitting, white, and off-white. In those suitcases Robinson carried twelve suits, five overcoats, and a hundred neckties, as well as all the other accompaniments. No one else in this group came even close to the Robinson inventory. Still, the Robinson traveling cast was trying to look as if they'd been there before. Most of them had not. "Be cool" were the watchwords. No one wanted to let on what an extraordinary moment this was. But it was a long way from Black Bottom.

Paris was a Valhalla of sorts for blacks, especially artists and entertainers. After Duke Ellington's 1939 European tour, the band leader gushed, "You can go anywhere and talk to anybody and do anything you like. It's hard to believe. When you've eaten hot dogs all your life and you're suddenly offered caviar it's hard to believe it's true."

During his time in France, Sugar Ray was so revered that he was given a French nickname: *Le Sucre Marvilleaux* (the Marvelous Sugar). Part of the reason for the adulation was Robinson's defeat of Jake La Motta, who had taken the middleweight crown from France's own Marcel Cerdan.

Another member of the entourage—and a key component in constructing the image of *Le Sucre Marvilleaux*—was the pink Cadillac. The car stopped traffic wherever it was seen in Paris. Sugar Ray was given a police escort wherever he went. "Whenever Sugar's fuchsia Cadillac convertible pulls away from the Claridge and heads up the Champs Elysées," it was reported, "grinning gendarmes wave ordinary traffic to a stop. Bicyclists swarm behind him, like gulls after a liner, happily shouting his name, 'Ehh-Ro-Bean-Song.'"

His earliest biographer, Gene Schoor, detected that Robinson, like so many blacks who had visited Paris before him, was taken by the lack of prejudice he encountered there. The famous actor Maurice Chevalier, as well as the boxer George Carpentier, hung around with Robinson while he was in France. Robinson welcomed all comers to his entourage, just as he did in the ring. The entourage was fluid, expanding outward like a puddle of champagne, and Sugar was generous with and without cause.

The best incarnation of such a group is when it represents the fulfillment of an obligation to friends and family who sacrificed extensively to propel the athlete to where he or she is. Membership into the entourage is the reward to the father who threw the ball back to you tirelessly after endless rebounds without taking a shot himself, to the mother who made sure you made it to every practice or had the money to pay the gym dues, and to the friends who fought for you—the one's who took the rap for you when *they* knew one of the gang did it, but they weren't sure who, and they were not going to let up until someone stepped up.

The presence of Robinson's entourage in Paris, along with their luggage, was but one example of his fidelity to those who had come up with him. Another exhibition of Robinson's loyalty was his continuing relationship with the then Alcatraz incarcerated Bumpy Johnson, the former king of the numbers rackets in Harlem. They were Harlem friends. Friendship was the key to this lifelong obligation. With little regard for his personal reputation and the harm that could be done to his commercial value by associating with Johnson and others, Robinson was determined to obtain permission to visit the notorious facility, and did so; in the end, he was praised in the press for this loyalty. This was yet another side of the enigmatic Robinson.

Such faithfulness can also lead to being taken advantage of by those who set about extracting as much as they could from the athlete. The constant threat of attack from within makes one's status in the group tenuous. Suspicions and jealousies can get a member of an entourage expelled. When the going gets tough, sometimes entourage members voluntarily depart. It was Robinson who accused Harry Wiley and George Gainford of deserting the entourage after he lost the 1955 Tiger Jones bout. When they left his camp after the loss, Robinson said, "Gainford and Wiley weren't walking out on me, they were walking out on my money. All these years they had lived off me, lived high, lived like millionaires, but now they thought there wasn't going to be any more money. They were deserting the sinking ship."

Of course, there were those who weren't intentionally milking the celebrity for large sums of cash, but their constant presence was difficult to understand. Often, members of the posse are not motivated entirely by selfishness or selflessness. Sugar Ray's was no exception. His entourage included all kinds.

In 1997, when Allen Iverson first entered the ranks of the National Basketball Association at the age of twenty-one, the major focus of the press was on the group of family and friends that were omnipresent. His entourage, and that of other young black men, began to be referred to as a posse. As much as it may have been used internally at the time, the application of the label *posse* grew to have predominantly negative connotations. The standard mode was to deny that your posse was your posse; you stood up tall and said that your friends were your friends and that loyalty was important above all else.

In addition to the hopes of the public, obligations are hoisted on athletes, both by their communities and by themselves. In a very practical way, Iverson's friends and family were focused on making sure that he would make it. They all recognized his skills early on and did all they could to insure that he was not harmed or held back.

Beyond the well-being of friends and family, the next obligation placed upon athletes is to invest in the community they left "back home." So many blacks can recall the number of "black dollar days" or admonitions to "buy black" they heard. We heard it regularly and knew how important it was to the black community. Although the concept of "recycling black dollars" in the community was the *eureka* idea of the 1960s and 1970s, it continues to surface as a panacea today. When emotionally worked up about this issue, black folks talk about the multiplier effect like Nobel Prize–winning economists.

Robinson practiced this reinvestment model; and although Robinson's commitment to his Harlem community was admirable, one must consider such actions in context. To a certain degree, Robinson had no choice but to open his empire in Harlem. After all, not many real estate agents or bank loan officers working in 1952 were going to help a young black man open up a barber shop or a lingerie boutique on Park Avenue. Robinson and the other black athletes of that era had no choice.

The reality, and ironically the biggest negative, of integration is choice. In the 1950s, Ray had no choice. His nightclub was where it had to be—in the black community. This was also true of Jack Johnson, Joe Louis, and later Wilt Chamberlain. They all, in their respective eras, had nightclubs in the black community.

Robinson was the first athlete to fully explore community reinvestment. Predecessors may have had a business or two, but Robinson had a small empire. He was able to be his own man, and he relished that role. Athletes with such business acumen are uncommon. Black athletes who exhibit or who are given credit for having business acumen are rarer still. Of athletes operating in major urban settings, Robinson had the fullest grasp of his business value. He also understood, better than almost everyone else who would find themselves in a similar position, that his value was highest while his career was at its peak. That's where Sugar Ray was unique. These were not retirement business ventures. These were businesses in full force at the peak of his athletic career.

Magic Johnson is the best exemplar of the Robinson tradition operating today. Even so, the true entrepreneur in Johnson emerged after his retirement and after his announcement in 1991 that he was HIV positive. He saw "Cap'n," his teammate Kareem Abdul-Jabbar, fall into financial disrepair in the mid-1980s. Jabbar's investments were largely limited partnerships, including hotels, restaurants, and a company that produced jump ropes. For the most part, Kareem had been investing his money without having much say in the business. On the other hand, Magic Johnson has a say in the smallest of details in the businesses he owns; he tries to use his intimate understanding of his clientele to safeguard his investment: "See, you've got to understand Black people. I know my customer base, because I'm it. I told Loew's, Black people are going to eat dinner at the movies—those hot dogs are our dinner. Same with the drinks. Our soda sales were just O.K. I said Black people love our flavored drinks, because we were raised on Kool-Aid. So we put in punch and strawberry soda and orange and the numbers went through the roof."

Consciously or not, Magic followed Robinson's example, or at least the example that Robinson set during the initial years of his business enterprises. Robinson, Magic, and other black and Latino athletes have all been confronted with the same issue: "What are you doing for your community?" Few have been able to answer that question in as positive a way as either Robinson or Magic. Magic's portfolio of investments is unique in that it includes bringing enterprises such as Loew's theatres, Starbucks, and T.G.I. Fridays to the black community. Strikingly, great white athletes such as Arnold Palmer, Jack Nicklaus, and Babe Ruth were rarely asked a similar question. Neither are the modern-day athletes; for them, the obligatory United Way commercial may be enough. Black athletes are expected to go so much further. A mere monetary contribution to a charity or an appearance in one of their commercials is just not enough.

Failure to invest or live in the black community can scar an otherwise solid image. When wealth motivates escape from the black community, the professional athlete is not the sole culprit. Flight has been the fate of other sectors of the black community ever since integration allowed those who could afford it to depart for better neighborhoods. But it is athletes who are most frequently pointed to as deserting the community.

After dealing with one's feelings of responsibility—those imposed internally and externally—to family, friends, and the community—the final obligation anyone who achieves even the most modest level of celebrity has to focus upon is charity. "I was born poor. I learned early what it was to need help. If God blessed me with the talent to make real big money then he also entrusted me with the responsibility to care for those without talent," Robinson wrote, laying out what, by his actions, amounted to a sincere commitment.

Giving money and time to charity is virtually a requirement for today's highly compensated athletes and entertainers. For some, it's sincere, but for others, it's what their handlers have directed them to do; for the rest, it's designed to clean up a previously unsavory image.

For Robinson, the media implied that his contributions were made to improve his public image. Robinson claimed that he was moved to support certain causes for more genuine reasons. His most publicized cause was the Damon Runyon Cancer Fund. In his autobiography he said that the loss of his childhood friend and fellow boxer, Louis Valentine, to cancer prompted his support of cancer research. He did not know much about cancer and felt that too little research had been done, so he gave to cancer research in memory of his friend. As it turned out, his oldest sister died from cancer as well.

Robinson became a spokesman for the Damon Runyon Cancer Fund, delivering checks to organizations and research institutions overseas and giving the proceeds of many bouts to the fund. The timing of his involvement with the fund and the fact that Dan Parker, the writer who wrote the desertion piece on Robinson, was the president of it, gave many reason to pause. But this was another realm where no one ever got the straight story from Robinson. He continued to support the fund as long as he had the wherewithal.

But Robinson had a true charitable spirit. On another occasion, he gave half a bout's purse, about $12,500, to the mother of Jimmy Doyle, the boxer who died in the ring from Robinson's punches. His giving to Jimmy Doyle's family eventually totaled around $20,000. Unlike Robinson, many athlete's make a point of keeping their giving quiet.

Even after his retirement and the collapse of his business empire, Sugar Ray continued to be active with charitable causes. After moving to Los Angeles, he started the Sugar Ray Robinson Youth Foundation with the support of Hollywood friends. He spent a good amount of time at the foundation's headquarters, where he spoke and joked with the kids, recounting experiences inside and outside the ring. Working with youth was his greatest love after boxing, and the memories of those children who passed through would testify to this. Many who would go on to amazing accomplishments spent their formative years at the Sugar Ray Robinson Youth Foundation, including the late Olympic sprint champion Florence Griffith-Joyner. She remembered her time spent there and said that it had a great impact upon her pride, confidence, and eventual success.

Friends, community, and broader charitable activities are challenges confronting all celebrities. The bigger your celebrity, the more difficult it is to chart the proper course in this sea of obligation. Missteps in this realm can catalyze a wide range of problems.

PART FOUR

ENDINGS

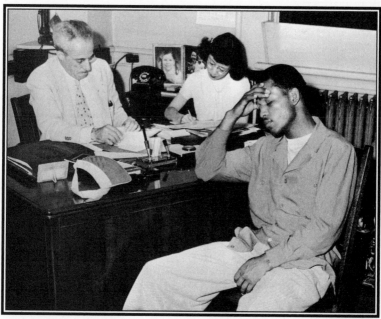

Sugar Ray at Coroner's inquest following the death of Jimmy Doyle, Cleveland, Ohio, June 27, 1947. Photo: Corbis.

CHAPTER EIGHT

PROBLEMS

"Mr. and Mrs. Sugar Ray Robinson!" Ed Sullivan exclaimed as he gestured out into the studio audience. Sullivan would routinely introduce the stars who were in the crowd. But this night there was a problem. The female asked to stand with Robinson was not his wife. She stood up anyway. Close friends sitting at home in front of their Philcos could only shake their heads.

"I was taught to obey the Ten Commandments," Robinson wrote, "and I have—except the one about adultery. I'm not proud of having broken it, but I'm neither saint nor sinner. I'm a gladiator."

Still, the only stories about Ray that reached the pages of the tabloids were those that really blew up—such as his appearance on the Sullivan show—or those he chose to reveal in his own autobiographical dispatches. It is fortunate for Ray, and other athletes of earlier eras, that the *National Enquirer*, the *Globe*, *Real Sports*, and *60 Minutes* were not yet on their trails. If such outlets had existed then, it is likely that far more stories of sex, substance abuse, and money woes would have tarnished the images of many more figures.

There is probably more about Robinson than his philandering that we don't know about and that we would not want today's young athletes to emulate. Robinson, like any man, had his shortcomings and he made his mistakes. The money and adulation afforded successful athletes can exacerbate a man's flaws by removing inhibitions and feelings of vulnerability. And the money is a magnet for those who deal in vices.

Certainly, inappropriate incidents with women seem to be the most publicized problems for male athletes. In this regard, occasionally sports magazines go beyond the box scores and the typical profiles to inform readers about the unseemly behavior of their heroes. One such example, perhaps the most notorious, was the decidedly unglamorous *Sports Illustrated* cover story titled "Paternity Ward." That article listed athletes who had fathered children with women they were not married to, and sometimes barely even knew. The story went on to report the ways in which the fathers would make deals both in and out of court to keep these stories under wraps.

Sugar Ray's first child was born on September 25, 1939. Robinson was eighteen years old and unmarried. The child was a boy named Ronnie Smith. Ray and his young girlfriend were naïve and too caught up in their developing bodies and raging hormones to think much about the repercussions of their actions. This was not an atypical story, and also in the mode of the day the couple married at the insistence of Robinson's mother. Today, money solves many of those problems. Marjorie Joseph was the first of Ray's three wives.

Ray would later recount how his mother had screamed at him: "'Junior, if you don't marry, you're going to get a record against you. You'll go to prison and that'll be on your record for the rest of your life. You got to get married.'" The key concern was that Ms. Joseph was a minor; there were fears that her family would bring charges for statutory rape. Eventually, the marriage was annulled; it lasted only three months. One writer determined that it was a divorce paid for by Robinson's original manager, Curt Horrmann.

Paternity claims would surface again during Robinson's career: Barbara Trevigne brought a paternity suit against Robinson claiming that he was the father of her six-year-old son. A court found in favor of Robinson even though he admitted he had been intimate with the woman.

As Ray II described to author Herb Boyd, it was not un-usual for Robinson to drive around Harlem to check his "traps," locations where he stashed female companions, at the Theresa Hotel, the Apollo, and elsewhere. Boyd again, writing with Ray II, was able to highlight the boldness with which some athletes carry out affairs. Near the end of their marriage, after Edna Mae had filed for separation in the early 1960s, Ray would still come around occasionally. On one such visit, he asked Edna Mae to prepare lunch for him. She did as asked without much thought. She still loved this man and didn't think one lunch was too much to ask—until she found out that the meal was to be eaten by Ray and his current paramour. "The man was incredible," she wrote in her diary that night.

Robinson's dalliances were heartbreaking for Edna Mae and those closest to the family, but they did not really alter the perception of the public. Like the later revealed John F. Kennedy and Marilyn Monroe stories, they were not publicized. A blind eye was turned to his extramarital affairs, and later to his divorces. Our culture's permissive attitude toward promiscuity would later come to haunt us with the onset of the AIDS epidemic. Magic Johnson brought into sharp focus the dangers of sexual promiscuity for professional athletes. When he announced he was HIV-positive, he explained that his condition was a direct consequence of his behavior. When the initial shock that swept through the country had subsided, Magic was able to provide a glimmer of hope and an example of how to live life with the deadly virus. He has been able to maintain his health as well as become a successful businessman.

Although Magic's exposed frailty made him more human, many an athlete has found himself ostracized as a result of his sexual misconduct. The wildly unpredictable and occasionally incoherent incarnation of Mike Tyson that exists today can largely be traced back to his rape conviction in 1992. Of course, Tyson had always appeared slightly unhinged, but his energy had been channeled toward the next fight and the winning of championships. After falling afoul of the law and public opinion, he has never achieved the success—either in or out of the ring—that he had prior to that incident. But amazingly, although otherwise unmarketable and with skills diminished, he continued to command unprecedented paydays for his ring appearances.

More recently, the NBA star Kobe Bryant was accused of having nonconsensual sex with a hotel employee at a Vail-area resort in Colorado. During the previous season, Bryant had received the most votes when the leagues fans cast ballots for the All-Star game. He had recently signed a $45 million endorsement deal with Nike; people were beginning to believe that he might just be the next Michael Jordan. Although the superstar would eventually be acquitted of the charges, his image would be forever tarnished; advertisers and supporters would flee as quickly as they had once flocked to him. The notion that a young black man might have raped a white woman opens up psychic scars on both sides of the race line.

Four hours after he was formally accused by the Colorado prosecutor, Kobe and his wife strolled on to a Staples Center stage. "I didn't force her to do anything against her will," Kobe Bryant tearfully told an audience of dozens, knowing that millions would watch him over and over again electronically.

"I sit here in front of you furious at myself, disgusted at myself for making a mistake of adultery." Bryant said, close to convincingly. He went on, "I love my wife with all my heart." Kobe then looked directly into the eyes of his wife, Vanessa, who sat by his side, and said, "You're a blessing. You're a piece of my heart. You're the air I breathe. And you're the strongest person I know. I'm so sorry for having to put you through this and having to put our family through this."

On some unconscious level he knew—like Sugar Ray— that cheating on one's wife was something that the public could forgive. Kobe would soon learn that transcendent performance could go a long way toward whitewashing away a man's sexual mistakes: his 81-point total in a single game against the Toronto Raptors in January 2006 did more for his rehabilitation than any amount of tears.

For those sitting on their couches in the comfort of their living rooms, it is quite easy (and sometimes appropriate) to cast dispersions on those young athletes who, at the very least, are guilty of getting themselves into bad situations. However, the constant travel from city to city without loved ones and the high esteem that so many members of the opposite sex have for these athletes make temptation ever present.

Besides sex, drug use is another illicit pastime available to these young men with expendable incomes and time to burn between bouts, matches, and games.

Two types of substance abuse have emerged amongst the athlete population, and each for different reasons. First, recreational drugs potentially see increased use, most often, because these young men and women have so much time on their hands along with money and opportunity. The aura of invincibility is again a factor. Those who have beaten the odds to reach the pinnacle of success will likely believe that they can again defy the odds by using drugs with impunity.

Addiction lays low the great ones just the same as it does car salesmen and substitute teachers. It is a societal problem that crops up in high schools and universities; many of the greatest athletes humbled by addiction have seen a friend or a family member struggle with similar demons but believed that the demons could not capture them. In this instance, the asserted responsibility of the athlete to be a role model makes their trespasses more noteworthy than those that occur every day in anonymity.

A media furor kicked up when Randy Moss, the star NFL receiver, told Bryant Gumbel on the HBO program

Real Sports in 2005, "I have used, you know, marijuana . . . since I've been in the league." Moss then tried to clarify his statement: "But as far as abusing it and, you know, letting it take control over me, I don't do that, no." But Moss would elaborate too much, as people often do when they've made an unwise statement: "I might have fun. And, you know, hopefully . . . I won't get into any trouble by the NFL by saying that, you know. I have had fun throughout my years and, you know, predominantly in the off season."

Even in this rare moment of candor, Moss, having some sense of the firestorm that would erupt around his remarks, added, "But, you know, I don't want any kids, you know, watching this taking a lesson from me as far as 'Well, Randy Moss used it so I'm going to use it.' I don't want that to get across. Like I say . . . I have used [marijuana] in the past. And every blue moon or every once in a while I might."

Randy Moss is a very rich man. More accurately, he is a very rich young man, and he is making the same mistakes that many young men make. He admits that occasionally he uses drugs, but he fails to consider the consequences, and possibly he doesn't care about them. In this regard, the specifics of his admission are not as important as the way in which they are made important because of his status in society.

Those who have written about Sugar Ray, including himself, claim that he did not drink or use drugs. In his autobiography he talks about the problems he saw his parents having with alcohol. He claims these early traumas made him swear that wine would never touch his lips: "It was alcohol consumption by both parents that led to their break-up."

Performance-enhancing substances are another form of illegal drug use for athletes. Anabolic steroids have gained widespread use over the years because athletes are always looking for a competitive edge. The pressure of success and the increasingly cutthroat competition have combined with the ready availability to increase use to epidemic proportions. Accusations have been made against NFL players, such as Lyle Alzado and Bill Romanowski; major league baseball sluggers, such as Mark McGwire and Barry Bonds; and track and field stars, such as Ben Johnson and more recently the bicyclists competing in the annual Tour de France.

Sugar Ray's strongest injections were an occasional shot of Vitamin B-12; and although Sugar Ray was not an abuser of steroids, he might have told you that he did know a thing or two about a modest form of "blood-doping." However, for Sugar Ray this meant a psychological rather than a chemical advantage. His consumption of beef blood is a staple of all the well-told stories about Robinson. Ferdie Pacheco, the fight doctor, marveled at this intimidating habit when describing a press luncheon before one of the La Motta fights:

On this occasion he decided to confront La Motta with a bit of bizarre behavior. As they sat next to each other . . . Robinson summoned the waiter.

"Would you ask the chef if I could have a glass of beef blood?" he inquired.

The waiter looked at Jake, who shrugged.

"Don't you know that the great Joe Louis drinks eight ounces of blood every day for three weeks before a fight?" Robinson asked his opponent.

"Oh," said La Motta, looking sick to his stomach, "what does that do for you?"

"It gives you strength for the last kick, rounds 10 to 15. Don't you see how strong Joe Louis is in the last rounds?" replied Ray.

Jake considered this information, then shook his head decisively. "Man, I don't need that. I'm not drinking no blood."

Sugar Ray smiled. He knew he had hooked a sucker; now he reeled him in. "Yeah, Jake, that's why I'm going to be beating your ass from 10 to 15. I'll be strong. You'll be weak."

La Motta shuddered again at the thought of swallowing blood. "Yeah, well, that is just a lot of shit. I ain't drinking blood!"

Thankfully for Sugar, it was relatively inexpensive to have a waiter bring out a glass of beef blood, but many athletes have seen their fortunes disappear to maintain their own habits—whether recreational or performance-

enhancing drugs, expensive cars, or child support pay-
ments from illicit affairs. Such money problems often occur because these young men and women indulge every
passing whim. As focused as they can be on the field, they
often exhibit a glaring lack of preparation or considera-
tion for how to live life away from the cheering fans.

Of course, this cavalier attitude can work while a player
is in the middle of his prime earning years. However, most
cannot have the longevity or job security enjoyed by
Roger Clemens, for example, who has been able to command an exorbitant salary while pitching into his forties.
Meanwhile, planning for retirement is a problem for the
entire work force, and most have decades to figure things
out. Most fumble around because they think they're too
young; they spend what little cash they have now and
make vague plans to start saving when they are in their
thirties. For sure, they believe, they'll play longer than the
average three years of other NFL players—but for most of
them it's an unlikely prospect. Apart from not making the
basic retirement investments, financial problems can be
magnified when an agent or financial manager without
qualifications or true loyalty is hired to manage the funds.

Robinson continued to fight until 1965—long after his
prime—because he needed the money. Robinson even
owed money to his longtime physician, Vincent Nardiello, who reportedly stopped speaking to Ray because
of the debt. Although Robinson did handle much of his
own business, he still relied on others to manage these

matters at various times throughout his career, often to his detriment.

When a young athlete who has coasted through his formal education puts too much faith in one person for guidance, the result can be disastrous. Unfortunately, today's players are often at the mercy of their agents, a result of the economics of professional sports in America. The wave of agent involvement in a player's decision making may have crested in 2005 on the front lawn of a former wide receiver for the Philadelphia Eagles, Terrell Owens.

Owens stood in the background, uncomfortable. Drew Rosenhaus, his agent, was speaking for him. It is typical for an athlete today to have a high-powered agent handle his "business." Theoretically, that is what Rosenhaus was doing. His hair was slicked back and he wore a solid tie on a solid shirt—well past the Regis Philbin *Millionaire* moment of style.

"Next question," the sports agent said before a huge throng of reporters, microphones, and cameras. He was responding to yet another reporter query about the man who stands behind him. Terrell Owens, better known as "T.O.," had just apologized for the second time for disruptive comments he had made about his team, specifically about Donovan McNabb, the star quarterback. The apology given that day would not make much difference in the minds of those who heard it because it was no secret that such an apology had been mandated by the franchise. Owens had caused a rift in the locker room and pitted teammate against teammate. The team that had been within one touchdown of winning the Super Bowl the season before was now tearing itself apart from within.

Still, both the player and the agent would tell you that the reason for all this commotion was that Owens deserved more money. Owens wanted to be paid what he thought he was worth, relative to other wide receivers in the league. The problem was that he had just signed his contract, and the Philadelphia Eagles are a franchise well known for not renegotiating contracts, particularly when a player makes a demand. T.O. famously played, terrifically, in the 2005 Super Bowl following a miraculous recovery from an ankle injury. No one thought he would be ready in time to play. Risking a more serious injury he played anyway, and he played well beyond anyone's expectations.

Rosenhaus was convinced that he could parlay Owens's spectacular showing in the Super Bowl into a more lucrative deal. He may not have fully contemplated an intransigent front office in Philadelphia and a loose cannon of a client. Soon these negotiations devolved into a full-scale melodrama that sunk a team's season and sabotaged the image of Owens. Much of the blame fell to the agent and his greed: the bigger the deal for the player the bigger the cut for the agent. Owens ended up with a new contract, but it was with a new team, the Dallas Cowboys.

In boxing, the same general rules apply when it comes to the fees of representation. The typical fee taken by managers, and it's provided for by law in some states, is one third of the fight purse. This money comes out of the net that trickles down after the promoter and the casinos get their cut from the cable concerns and networks, which put the bulk of the funds into the boxing system. The major difference between football and boxing fees is not in the basic system but in the percentages: The typical football agent receives only 3 percent of a football player's salary. With so much more of the money going directly into the player's coffers, there is far less incentive for an NFL player to control his own business. Low single-digit percentages are typical in the other major sports as well. Boxing, again, is the exception.

To say that Sugar Ray was inspired to control his own businesses would be a gross understatement; he was praised and chastised in equal parts for the meticulous control he tried to keep over his ring dealings. Sugar Ray could be so obsessed with getting himself the best possible deal that he often mishandled one important element of his celebrity. His hard-line business practices could occasionally alienate fans, and they certainly did not endear him to boxing promoters. The press reports for several years were negative about Robinson. As *Time* magazine reported: "Robinson seemed determined to make himself the most unpopular man in the ring. He snapped at sportswriters, took to running out on promoters, got a reputation as a cold, calculating type, with an icy 'What's-in-it-for-me?' attitude to every thing."

T.O. would make similar mistakes many years later. With the increased coverage of the business side of sports, T.O.'s image and possible endorsement dollars have been diminished. There is ample evidence that Owens was right in claiming he was underpaid. Many around the league considered him the most dominant player at his position. However, the way that he went about trying to secure his pay increase undermined his standing with the fans and ultimately with the team's ownership. By becoming so obsessed with receiving what he perceived as fair value he managed to lower his value in the eyes of everyone else. He appeared petulant and greedy, whereas months before he had been selfless and courageous. Of course, it's difficult to know how much of the public face was T.O.'s own doing and how much was related to his agent's guidance.

Apart from appearing overbearing in business dealings, the quickest way to lose the sympathy of a fan base is to squander one's good fortune once it has been amassed. Unfortunately, anyone who made a noise about his business dealings was bound to have a few folks from Washington paying special attention, so it should not be a big surprise that Robinson's most publicized money problems were with the Internal Revenue Service.

For once Sugar Ray was not the trailblazer: The saddest public battle against the IRS was waged by Joe Louis. Long after he should have retired, Louis was forced to continue fighting to pay off his debts; he would eventually lose the title to Rocky Marciano. In a scene right out of *Requiem for a Heavyweight*, and to the shame of all who loved him, he had to become a professional wrestler to make ends meet. In that last ring episode, Louis's heart muscles were damaged when a three-hundred-pound wrestler by the name of Rocky Lee went well beyond the script of the evening and stepped on the chest of the once great American champion.

"I was threatened with foreclosures on my mortgages. My taxes were unpaid. My stock portfolio was virtually worthless," Robinson told Dave Anderson. According to the man who was managing his entertainment career, Joe Glaser:

> I was the one who was responsible for it being found out. When Robinson got back from his dancing tour he came to me in desperate condition. The banks were foreclosing on him—he even had a $9,000 mortgage on his house that he was in trouble over.
>
> Well, I went up to his office and looked over his business statements. He had six businesses going and not one of them was making money. The books were in a mess. I don't think an accountant could straighten them all out. But they did show that there was at least $250,000 missing. At least.

The main reason that Sugar Ray was able to overcome most of the negative imagery of these issues was that he fought—for the most part at the highest level—for twenty more years. On the other hand, O. J. Simpson, for example, couldn't get back on the field after his murder trial, and Mark McGwire couldn't stride into the batter's box again after his unsatisfactory turn as witness in Washington, D.C. Meanwhile, Kobe was able to score 81 points in a game. His redemption was underway.

That Robinson survived all his missteps is a testament to his talent and perseverance, but it doesn't undo the mistakes—innocent or otherwise—that he made. Whether in business or family, Sugar Ray did not always make the best decisions. He retired to an increasingly run-down part of Southern California rather than to the French Riviera. Still, his image never lost its luster for long, and no one could ever forget that he was The Champ.

CHAPTER NINE

DEATH

Sugar Ray Robinson lived his final years in a lime-green duplex located at Tenth Avenue and West Adams Boulevard in the Crenshaw district of Los Angeles. These were once grand homes in the southwest section of the city. The dwellings had names such as "The Winfandel House." The mansion that houses memorabilia from the 1932 Los Angeles Olympics, is a few blocks east on Adams. Powerful black churches, including Holman Methodist, where the civil rights veteran the Reverend Joseph Lowery presided for years, is nearby.

Some of the first black actors in Hollywood, those who played the maids and servants in the big studio productions, had made their home in this part of town. Ray and his third wife, Millie, lived upstairs in the unit above

Wright Filmore, the owner. On every side of the duplex there were decorative security bars on both levels. The curved metal was painted white, as were the wrought iron railings guiding the cement double flight of stairs up to the second level. The shrubbery and lawn were landscaped in the sparse Southern California style. Inside the Robinson house, visitors were greeted with a glass case displaying the boxer's championship boxing belts.

Ray's home was located just up from Johnny's Pastrami, around the corner from Leo's Barbecue and Baker's Tacos (where you could get five for 99 cents). Dinner at the Robinson home, in this final era, was almost always spicy food. Tacos—homemade and not from nearby Baker's— were one of his favorites and, according to Ray, Millie made the best. On other occasions you were likely to be served savory ham hocks and collard greens.

Like the rest of Los Angeles, this was an automobile neighborhood. The only times you would find large groups of people on the street, other than those waiting for their orders at Johnny's or Baker's, was when church was letting out.

Further up the street were the places where Ray would hang out. One was Jerry's Flying Fox, on Santa Barbara Boulevard, which later became Martin Luther King Boulevard. He was a regular on Friday nights when they were serving gumbo. A few blocks away was Marla's Memory Lane in Leimert Park (owned by the actress Marla Gibbs), where Ray, Millie, and friends would go to hear O. C. Smith sing "God Didn't Make Little Green Apples." With his own establishment in Harlem nothing more than a memory, these jaunts throughout Los Angeles served as modest substitutes.

He also spent a lot of time in Beverly Hills and Hollywood. He'd hold court at tables in Matteo's and other famous hotspots. In spite of all that had changed since his heyday, the celebrities would still flock to him. As one of his close friends put it, he was the "Celebrity's Celebrity."

These evenings out on the town often ended at the cocktail lounge in the Bel-Air Hotel. When Ray walked in, the piano player would usually break into "When My Sugar Walks Down the Street" or "Here's to You Mrs. Robinson."

In the daytime, brightly colored aloha shirts became a staple of Ray's wardrobe. Even if the clothes had changed, the championship smile was still ever present. Another amendment to Ray's visage was the unfamiliar paunch above his belt. The bulge was not extreme—Ray still had a physique that most middle-aged men would have envied—but this was not the version of Ray that the world was accustomed to seeing. His weight now hovered around 180 pounds.

His hair was still immaculate, but it would begin to have a bit of gray around the neck and temple at the end of the week as the dye began to fade. During this time, Ray's mental acuity was beginning to fade as well. Millie sought to deliver the familiar to him, to make him feel comfortable and competent, and one of the most familiar places was the barbershop.

When Ray and Millie headed to the barbershop—in his final years his wife would take him to one of several shops in the area—they would slowly walk out to the Cadillac, which had "SUG N ME" personalized California license plates, parked on Tenth Avenue. Millie would have to help him sit on the passenger side. He could no longer drive his Ford Pinto with the "1 CHAMP" plate.

Millie became very protective of her husband; she did not want anyone to see him suffering from Alzheimer's disease. She kept almost everyone away from Sugar Ray, from the press to prospective entourage members. In documentaries years later, Ray's family members—including his sons and his sister Evelyn—would universally complain that Millie limited their access to him. Even his own mother had difficulty getting to him.

As Ray moved into the twilight of his life he was not caught unaware by the figure of death. He was more familiar with mortality than most men. His deepest association with death was Jimmy Doyle's 1947 death in the ring. In the hours before that fight, Ray had told anyone who would listen that he "had a dream last night that I killed Doyle." Only a fool would have believed him. Nevertheless, Ray was convinced that fate had decided he was going to kill Doyle in the ring. He wanted the fight to be called off. Jimmy Doyle died seventeen hours after his fight with Ray.

Ray's response to a query about whether or not he knew Doyle was in trouble was telling, but true: "It's my business to get him in trouble," Sugar Ray said with a raspiness that added depth to the otherwise high-pitched voice.

Heading into the 1960s, and as the boxing career was ending, Robinson had boxed in twenty-one world championship fights. He had fought the equivalent of several great careers after the Doyle fight, and he had done it all with one eye on the inevitable end. But the end for Robinson evolved into a moving target. After all those fights and spotlights, Ray's body couldn't keep up with his wits. As his trainer, Gainford, said in the final fights, "Oh my God, look at that man. He can do nothing anymore." According to Ali at the end of his own career: "I could see the shot coming, but I couldn't block it fast enough. I could see an opening for a punch, but by the time my brain sent the message to my hand to move, the opportunity was no longer there." Five of Robinson's nineteen career losses came in the final six months of his career, after he had turned forty-four.

One of Robinson's final bouts was against an unremarkable boxer, Young Joe Walcott. Walcott was no relation to Jersey Joe, the former heavyweight world champion; Young

Joe had poached the name. A reporter had queried Young Joe, "The papers say you have a 6–10–2 record. That right?" He could only respond with an "uh-huh." Robinson won. He fought Young Joe Walcott in three of his last nine fights.

After Ray had reached to these depths for opponents, even those who had the most belief in him and the most to profit from him felt obligated to tell him to call it a career. Some of the most stirring words that put Robinson on the path to that retirement night in the Garden came from Miles Davis, the celebrity who found his celebrity style in Robinson. After a poor performance in one of those last fights, Miles came into the musty dressing room. In a gravelly whisper he said, "Ray, you're packing it in."

After one forgetful fight with Young Joe Walcott, Larry King, then a young reporter, heard Robinson call out from the showers to Gainford, "Hey, George! What was that cat's name I fought tonight?" The "old" younger Sugar Ray never would have taken a fight so lightly—he may not have paid much more mind to the opponent, but he always had the utmost respect for the sanctity and potential lethality of the fight itself.

In the end, not only did he fight in such places as Tijuana, Steubenville, and Johnston, but some nights he made only a couple of thousand dollars. On the worst nights he made a few hundred. Before these fights, there was no longer a police escort to lead him into the ring, and the entourage had gone as well. Gritty characters such as Mashky McGhee, a gofer, would simply yell into a blood-stained, cement-floored dressing room, "Let's go."

This final incarnation of Sugar Ray Robinson the boxer imparted one last lesson to those who would follow. When being confronted by the press after a loss, Ray would never make excuses. As for what happened in the ring, he felt that alibis were wrong and always tried to take the blame for his own performances. In spite of the increased frequency of poor outings, the glimmer of hope remained for some time—held onto just as much by Ray as by the public.

One of the last fights where the Robinson fans and dreamers realistically thought he could pull it off was against Gene Fullmer. Fullmer was ten years his junior. They had fought twice before, trading victories. Those who believed that Ray had a chance to vault himself back into contention held onto the fact that he was close in his final fight with Joey Archer. Still, this fight was against Fullmer—a man equal to any of Robinson's greatest rivals.

The final Fullmer fight was held at the Las Vegas Convention Center in 1961. Oddly, both men wore white trunks. Robinson wore white trunks with red stripes; Fullmer wore white trunks with black stripes. Sugar Ray's cornermen, George Gainford and Harry Wiley, wore what looked like varsity high school sweaters, with three white stripes on the right sleeves.

Robinson was the clear fan favorite insofar as his introduction was greeted with fewer boos than his opponent's. Fullmer was entering the ring with a living legend, and the crowd was pulling for the past and present hero. Desertion, arrogance, womanizing, and all the other negatives were diminished by the marvelous effort and public presence. A Robinson victory might help some in those cramped seats reclaim their own past glory, a piece of their youth, but a Robinson defeat would just signify the end of an era.

The referee for the bout is the veteran Frankie Carter of San Francisco. During the handshake at the center of the ring, he gives the usual instructions, and then adds, "All I say is stop, box or break." Carter pauses, then says, "Unless I need to say some more." The slightly confusing comments are met by the stony silence of the two pugilists at the center of the ring.

As they stand, about to touch gloves at the close of instructions, it's striking how heavily greased Fullmer's face is. No Vaseline was spared in an effort to insure that grazing punches from Robinson slide off harmlessly. It is the understanding in Fullmer's corner that Robinson's blows are likely to be inaccurate. The younger Robinson would have landed his punches squarely and no amount of Vaseline could have lessened the impact.

The Las Vegas Convention Center uses a ringing bell to start the fight. When the bell sounds, no one moves.

They all look at each other and try to figure out whether or not they should get under way. Once the referee figures it out, he waves Robinson and Fullmer in.

Fullmer keeps his hands close together in front of his face. It is a bit of a peek-a-boo style. He looks very solid from the opening bell and is working to get inside on Robinson. Fullmer is focused on Robinson's body. The strategy is clear: Pound at the aging body and wear him down. Fullmer has the utmost respect for his forty-year-old opponent; he has no visions of knocking Robinson out. The heat had managed to take him down in the Maxim fight, and many thought that only such a force of nature could put him down again. So Fullmer just hopes to wear Robinson down and get him to the point where he can do no harm. This has become the strategy for the talented boxers facing Robinson in these twilight years.

The fight is being tightly contested, both combatants playing conservatively and viciously. Neither boxer misses an opportunity to throw a punch in a clinch. At the end of the first, there's no stopping at the bell. At this early stage of the bout, it's a moment that resembles the Valentine Golden Gloves bout. They flail at the very end.

Don Dunphy, the announcer on the Gillette television broadcast, informs fans that the bell was more like an alarm clock. In rounds one and two the boxers are slow in getting started because they are unfamiliar with the tone. Referee Carter continues to wave the boxers in as they fail to react.

In round two, Robinson is throwing strong jabs followed by combinations. He clinches and then moves
away again, trying to maximize his points while taking as
little heat as possible. At the end of round two, Fullmer
finds a bit more of Robinson but makes no great strides.
Robinson comes on with strong combinations at the end
of the round. In the next round, Fullmer uses a defensive
stance, one that Ken Norton would later use to block the
blows from Ali. Robinson comes inside and Fullmer lands
multiple punches. These hurt Robinson. While bearing
the brunt of Fullmer's attack, Robinson does manage to
draw blood from Fullmer's left eye. Perhaps Robinson has
chosen to take a few shots to deliver some punishment.
But even if this is an intentional ploy, longtime Robinson
watchers cringe. In years past, Robinson could deliver the
blows without having to take them.

Drawing blood from Fullmer comes at a price. Even
though he is now staining the canvas, he is consistently all
over Robinson. Sugar Ray is on the ropes in round three,
and it appears that he could be going down at any moment. A bloodied but confident Fullmer is permanently
shifting the momentum in his favor.

When the bell rings to end the round, no one hears it.
It is ringing almost in rhythm with Fullmer's unrelenting
blows, and for maybe a dozen seconds no one besides
George Gainford and Harry Wiley seems to notice. When
it becomes apparent that the referee does not hear it, they
climb over that second rope as rapidly as they can, step

between Robinson and Fullmer, and pull their man out of the ring. Partially to blame for the problems with the bell is the crowd: Few have ever seen Robinson in that kind of trouble before and the torrent of noise raises exponentially with their awe, confusion, and excitement. As the warning whistle sounds for round four, just before the bell, Robinson is still groggy from the beating of the last round. Nevertheless, he knows he has to get back out there.

At the beginning of the fourth round, Fullmer decides not to go aggressively after the boxer ten years his senior. He lays back, seemingly biding his time. This gives Robinson time to catch his breath. Now, Robinson begins to do the things that great boxers can do: He doesn't give in. If there is anything to the stories he told about beef blood, this is a fight where the unique meal may provide an edge. To have any chance at victory, he has to gather the strength from somewhere within to go another twelve rounds.

Fullmer remains cautious as Robinson's movements start to speed up. Robinson is delighted to see that stool come out to end round four. The cut men for Fullmer do a good job in the middle rounds of keeping the gash over his eye closed, but Robinson goes back to work on it in each round. Both boxers seem to be one well-timed blow from defeat, or from victory.

Round ten is just another turning point in this era of boxing. It is in round ten that the mild cut above Robinson's left eye appears, in the same location as the one that

Fullmer has been forced to nurse for most of the bout. The blood of the two boxers begins to mix on their gloves, on the canvas, on their faces, and in their mouths.

The entire ring and all inside it are slick with blood and sweat. Just as the announcer says that the boxers are coasting, Fullmer makes another one of his patented charges forward. It is at this stage of a bout that each fighter must rely on his training—both mentally and physically. In round eleven, Fullmer again charges aggressively. Fullmer is obviously searching for the full five points for this round. The scoring is on a five point must (the winner of the round *must* be awarded five points by the scorers and the losers four points or fewer). He had Robinson pinned in his corner early on, scoring with multiple blows. Robinson is best when he dances away, but fatigue keeps bringing both fighters into the clinch. In this round, they spend a lot of time rabbit punching each other to the head with short choppy blows. They are in too tight to do any real harm to each other.

Fullmer's peek-a-boo defense is starting to show holes. He began the fight covering up at nose level, but at this point his defense is down to the bottom of his chin and shoulders. Still, Fullmer hits Robinson right up through the end of the round and finally lands a blow that staggers him. Fullmer sees the opening, but the bell sounds as he starts to move forward.

In round twelve, Robinson moves rapidly at his foe but cannot deliver any combinations of note. Soon, both boxers go back to the clinch, fatigued. During the last forty-five seconds of the round, they look as though they want to separate and get back to boxing; but before the round ends, they are back in each other's grasp again. These are long seconds. The three-minute rounds seem like an eternity in the final rounds, even for the fans. There is often booing because of boxer inaction.

In round thirteen, it is more of the same. Fullmer connects on a few blows to Robinson's head, but most of the battling is in tight once again. The boos gather force with each clinch. Punches continue to be exchanged, neither boxer getting much of the best of the other. When they do, the other boxer comes back and evens it up.

Both men weighed a little over 159 pounds at the beginning of the bout, but each is probably at least a half dozen pounds lighter now from loss of fluids. Both are determined not to go down. The only physical advantage Robinson has is an inch in height over the five-foot-ten Fullmer. But the ten-year age difference is a greater disadvantage than a negligible difference in height or reach.

Fullmer's cut man, Angelo Curley, is responsible for keeping him in the fight for the fifteenth and final round. Many fights have been lost by the better boxer because a referee or doctor decides too much harm is being done by a gushing wound. On television the advertising image on the screen for the final round is the old Alka-Seltzer mascot. Both men are aching, and both would savor something more powerful than a seltzer.

They both dig down deep in the last thirty seconds. Adrenalin throws the punches. They both leave it all in the ring, and neither can deliver that final knockout blow. You have to beat the champion, and in this battle the champion to start the day is Fullmer. Glimpses of the Robinson of the past are there, but the years have caught up with him. Glimpses may not be enough to give him the victory. No one strains to hear the final bell, and the boxers semihug at center ring.

In Las Vegas, two judges and the referee score the bout. Cards are being added and there was an uncertainty. Don Dunphy expresses his doubt in the television broadcast. The fans murmur, but there was no overt cheering for either boxer. It must be close.

The ring announcer, Dick Porter reads the cards:

"70–64, Fullmer."

"70–67, Fullmer."

"70–66, Fullmer."

It's a unanimous decision. In the postfight interview, Fullmer said in a remarkably unstressed voice, "I was glad that I fought Robinson past his prime." He went on to tell him what a great fighter Robinson was.

Following the Fullmer loss, Robinson's cornermen began telling reporters that the referee was out of line, that he'd never call another fight of theirs, that "he stole the fight." These claims fly in the face of the unspoken rule that the true professional lives by, that is, never allow the competition to be close enough for an official to be able to make the call. In basketball, lead by more than a basket; in football by more than one score; in boxing, win by a knockout. If you don't do so, you might lose, and all the complaining in the world won't make a bit of difference on the final scorecard.

After taking in the claims of the cornermen, the reporter looked to Robinson to get his opinion.

"Ray?"

"I got no alibi. No plans, no alibi. I been fighting a long time. They pay on win and lose. He won."

The final question of the evening went to Robinson: "What do you think cost you the fight?"

"One thing. Fullmer."

In these twilight years, Robinson the competitor wanted one last title, and many in the wider world wanted one for him, too. Four years after the Fullmer loss, in his last fight, in Pittsburgh on November 10, 1965, he found the strength somewhere to battle Joey Archer, the number one middleweight contender, toe-to-toe until his body just gave out. As in the Fullmer bout, Robinson was a few blows, or one great one, from victory and from adding an exclamation point to the legend. Had he won, Robinson would have been positioned for yet a final title bout. He was then forty-four years old. He lost that final decision.

He had fought fifteen times in that final year of his career. He had lost nine times.

At a Pittsburgh airport interview, Ray wore a hip-length black leather jacket. His face was unscathed from the fight; every hair was in place. He made it clear to the reporters that at his age, and after that final valiant effort, he was retiring.

"But we have this offer of a return bout with Archer," a voice from what was left of the entourage blurted. Robinson was having none of it.

"Aw, what would be the point?"

We expect a victory from our greatest athletes, but it is the exception when the last at bat is a Ted Williams home run. More often than not careers end like Michael Jordan's: a forgettable final season with the Washington Wizards in 2003. His was a career that should have ended with the winning shot that all expected him to make in his last NBA championship game with the Chicago Bulls.

How can you quit when it is your passion? How can you quit when the adulation encourages you to go on? How can you quit when the afterlife is such a mystery, and your current reality is a dream? Why can't they all retire the way Jim Brown did, on the set of the *Dirty Dozen*, and leave us wondering what else they could have done and not watching how far they have fallen?

Robinson was his own worst enemy because he had so much faith in his own success and business sense. He saw boxing as the yet-to-be invented ATM. He gave money to family, friends, and those with sad stories—he fulfilled those obligations—because he felt blessed to be able to earn large amounts of money in the ring. It was this belief that added to his deafness to the final bell and encouraged him to be loose with his money. He was not destined to have a Jim Brown *Dirty Dozen* press conference retirement.

Like so many boxers, Robinson was a shell of himself in his waning years. Robinson's debilitation was increasingly evident in those final years of being ritually introduced at Las Vegas championship bouts—still one last payday for entering the ring. The first and second ropes had to be held down, and Robinson was gently guided through. The young, athletic, cool Sugar had made that entry effortlessly throughout his career and in early retirement. Dave Anderson writes that the signs of Robinson's final illness were evident long before the public was aware of it. Anderson jokingly reminisced about telling Ray, as he faltered in one of the long recording sessions, that he couldn't be tired after having endured those long bouts with La Motta.

In his book *Sugar Ray Robinson: Beyond the Boxer*, Sheldon M. Schiffman, the one-time president of the Sugar Ray Robinson Youth Foundation, described an incident showing how Alzheimer's hit Robinson. At an annual event for the Sugar Ray Robinson Youth Foundation, Ray was called on to give remarks at two points in the program. Ray made it through the opening remarks just fine. Then he was scheduled to introduce the keynote speaker mid-way through the program. Ray opened his notes and began to read from those same opening remarks. Ray had not a clue, but his close friend recognized what was happening. Schiffman went to the podium, joined Ray, and said, "You've got to let me say a few words about our guest of honor." At this point, the smallest matters were micromanaged by Millie and a few close friends. Under Millie's guidance he soon ceased all public appearances.

Other than George Foreman, who took at least a decade-long layoff from boxing, there are few prominent boxers of the latter half of the century who walked the earth without some indication that the game had gotten the best of them. Boxing victims include Louis, Ali, Joe Frazier, and Jerry Quarry. Sugar Ray Leonard, the aforementioned Foreman, and a few others, are marvelous exceptions.

Paralleling boxing, whether from injury to limbs, head, or otherwise, the football list of debilitated former greats is fairly extensive as well: Lyle Alzado, Bo Jackson, Gale Sayers, Steve Young, and Troy Aikman. It is the apparent mental toll on boxers that magnifies our view of their debilitation.

Maybe the saddest sight for a generation of Ali fans was that fight with Larry Holmes on October 3, 1980. Holmes was a one-time sparring partner for Ali, but that night the thirty-eight-year-old Ali looked like an old man compared to his relatively spry opponent. As Ralph Wiley wrote, Ali was "outquicked" on every jab, punch, feint, and counter. It wasn't supposed to happen, although we all knew that it would. As Wiley said, "After that night, I knew that in this life, anything can happen, given time." It was an eleven round TKO for Holmes, and the outcome could easily have been worse.

If that was not the saddest, then it had to be his shaky lighting of the Olympic torch in Atlanta in 1996. This was the new Ali, the re-crafted Ali that all of America loved without concern for politics or race. His life and transitions in the world had been the equivalent of Robinson's Damon Runyon contributions. He had been re-created, but the sight we saw, which enamored many, shocked his true lifelong fans.

Although less publicly than Ali, Sugar Ray, like so many boxers, suffered from the cruel punishment tied to pugilism. Robinson was diagnosed with Alzheimer's disease, but his disease was boxing. His debilitation was not as visible as Joe Louis's. He never became a celebrity greeter at a Las Vegas casino: Many witnessed that sadder and sadder sight in the last days of the Brown Bomber's life. Millie shielded Ray from that level of public display. It was only the occasional reporter or those who caught a glimpse of him in barbershops or at celebrity events that had an understanding of how the illness had taken its toll. He died at Brotman Memorial Hospital in Culver City,

California, on April 12, 1989. He was sixty-seven. The *New York Times* said the cause of death was Alzheimer's and diabetes.

On April 19, 1989, at 11:00 A.M., Robinson's funeral was scheduled to begin. Mike Tyson was one of the early speakers: "Some of us, we worry about where we're going when we die." Tyson, at the height of his notoriety, was on the verge of saying something provocative. "I'm sure heaven is asking him to come in with open hands," the not yet facially tattooed Tyson lisped. Then, this new era celebrity athlete broke down. "Thank you. I'm sorry. Really, excuse me." A photo of Robinson, framed in white lilies, was to the left of Tyson.

Not surprisingly, it was Jesse Jackson who delivered the eulogy that day. During the past few decades, the Reverend Jesse Jackson has been on the dais when a prominent black person has died. "Whenever he fought the world had a way of standing still. The center of the ring belonged to him," he told the audience, his robes flowing and his arms outstretched. Jackson's robes, for some reason, looked more valedictorian than preacher. The mourners sobbed audibly.

This funeral, in a way, did signify a special moment. The death of Robinson in 1989 was the passing of one of the last great celebrities of an earlier era. "Jesse Owens, Joe Louis, Jackie Robinson, Sugar Ray Robinson—the magnificent four. Sugar, Mr. Personality, boxer, negotia-

tor, actor, entrepreneur, pretty, sweet, tough." Jackson
had studied Robinson well.

"He was as authentic to America as Jazz. Sugar Ray
Robinson was an original art form. He took us beyond
racism and fear. He wasn't just a boxer. Sugar took care of
the people; God will take care of Sugar." Jackson's words
comforted all, famous, family, and fans.

Before the service, fans hung on the fence surrounding
the church. They reached for copies of the funeral program like children reaching for their share of food at the
back of a famine relief truck. They reached like the Birmingham Barons fans seeking Michael Jordan autographs
at Hoover Metropolitan Stadium. But not all the admir-
ers made it into the packed sanctuary.

"Champions win events, heroes win people. Champions are of short duration—you can be stripped of champion stature. Heroes cannot be. Heroes are needed. They
give us security and confidence. Sugar had charisma and
special gifts from God," Jackson preached. These words
seemed to capture the essence of Sugar Ray's life.

Robinson was not Mickey Mantle, and his illness and
death had been private; there was no critical commentary about *his* life. Rather, the words that day could
almost have been crafted by Robinson himself, and nothing would have pleased him—the consummately image-
conscious showman—more.

"He was part of the American quilt. His patch in that
quilt had nonnegotiable integrity. . . . He was born on

the bottom, but left on the top. He went from the 'gut-termost' to the 'uppermost.'" Jackson did not make the direct reference to Black Bottom, but he knew where Robinson had come from.

The five-thousand-seat cathedral that sits across the Crenshaw strip had not yet been built. The 2,500 mourners in attendance filled every space in the star-studded sanctuary. This was less than a mile from Robinson's Tenth Avenue home. A few blocks up from Leo's Barbecue, right near where Dick Barnett's "Fall Back Baby" billiards parlor was located. Before all these businesses had appeared, and before the invasion of the US car industry by names such as Datsun and Toyota, this was a strip where you could visit car lots and find the best deal on a Chevy or a Pontiac.

At one point during the service, Don King's familiar unstylish afro bobbed up above the other heads when Jackson told a story about Robinson's arrival in Europe along with his entourage. "Eat your heart out, Don King!"

When the end comes, legend takes over. Hopefully, or maybe not, the further we get away from the debilitated celebrity's death, the more we remember the young virile star. But nowadays, the media makes the image of the aging celebrity last longer. Exposure today goes way beyond the clips of an ailing Lou Gehrig or Babe Ruth saying farewell. We don't just see those clips on movie house newsreels on a single occasion, either. With Ali, for example, we see his decline many times each week. Although his decision to stay in the public eye is partly responsible, modern-day media access has much to do with it. Sugar Ray escaped most of that image-altering period—and Millie had much say in that.

Photo by Gordon Parks/Time Life Pictures/Getty Images, 1951.

Epilogue:
On Being
Sugar Ray

I saw Sugar Ray Robinson frequently in the early 1970s while I was in high school and working summers in the snack bar at Centinela Park in Inglewood, California. The Sugar Ray Robinson Youth Foundation was just getting underway back then. Robinson would come through smiling, waving, and checking on his kids. We'd see him feigning blows with kids and cracking jokes in that raspy voice.

We all knew who he was, me and my high school coworkers. We'd seen him on Thursday and Friday night boxing shows as little kids, not yet ten years old. More recently, we'd seen him on countless variety shows, such as the *Steve Allen Show*, and in bit parts in everything from the *Danny Thomas Show* to the Frank Sinatra movie *The Detective*.

We knew he was a *bad man*, and that we should hold him in awe the way we did Ali. Our fathers had told us so. This was so even if he was still wearing a process while we were all taking pride in forking out the largest afros we could. Yes, the conk was still in great shape. He was still fit and regularly hitting the Main Street Gym. He had not made the money that today's athletes make. No one did back then. In some ways, he went about as far as his money could carry him. He certainly might have delivered a different set of lessons had he made $100 million over his career rather than $4 million. Then again, he may have run through that much, too. Mike Tyson did.

Sugar Ray Robinson saw the world framed between two boxing gloves, and he took it on. His fame was so great, and his name so respected, that—as those who saw the movie *Ray* now know, bluesman Ray Charles Robinson shortened his own name, not only to avoid public confusion but to show deference to the greater celebrity. In the postwar 1940s and tumultuous 1950s, Sugar Ray Robinson was the world's top sports icon, black or white. Broadcast ratings for his bouts in the 1950s rivaled those of *I Love Lucy*, the perennial favorite of the times. Robinson was a great boxer, but he was also something more.

Not all athletes have the right goals beyond success on the field of play. One was O. J. Simpson. "When I was a kid growing up in San Francisco," O. J. told the *New*

Yorker magazine, "Willie Mays was the single biggest influence in my life. I saw how he made white people happy. I wanted to be like Willie Mays." Athletes have long observed each other, but not necessarily for the right reasons.

O. J. made white people happy for a long while. That was until his entry into the criminal justice system reminded them, and him, that he was black. He was not true to who he really was and, in dramatic fashion, he was exposed as people—even celebrities—wearing masks often are.

Not all athletes—no matter what their race—have learned all the lessons Sugar Ray Robinson had delivered via his positive as well as his negative experiences. Some followed a few, even if they did not consciously realize what they were doing, or that Sugar Ray had led the way. A 1951 *New York Times* headline reveals Robinson's exceptional edge in this segregation-integration transition era—and it wasn't designed to make white people happy:

SUGAR RAY GIVES MME. AURIOL KISS

The article began: "Sugar Robinson, the *Negro* middleweight boxing champion, kissed the wife of the President of France four times today—twice on each cheek." This kiss by Robinson was a sharp detour from Joe Louis, who had followed the instructions of his handlers never to be seen or photographed with a white woman, and definitely never to kiss one.

Robinson's rarefied status allowed him to live under different rules. The kiss was all part of Robinson's cool. He had a stylish nonchalance combined with arrogance, sexiness, and violence. Each of these traits, in the unique combination that Robinson possessed, was admired across the color line. Cool trumped race. *These* Sugar Ray characteristics were genuine. He was a new kind of celebrity.

Robinson, like many in his generation, often lived in two worlds—one black and one white. The black press's take on the kiss was typified in an *Ebony* magazine spread. It featured multiple pictures of Robinson kissing, observing, and dancing with white women. The only slightly negative commentary came from Edna Mae. After reporting that Robinson had lost his bout and title to Randy Turpin because he had been "playing" in Paris, the article went on: "His wife, Edna Mae—left behind in the States while Ray 'toured' Paris—summed up Ray's defeat while crying bitterly at the ringside: 'It would have been different if Ray had fought him before he went to Paris.'"

This was 1951, yet no one seemed distraught at the news of the kiss. It was just Sugar Ray Robinson kissing a white woman four years before schools in America were legally desegregated, four years before the grizzly lynching of Emmett Till for whistling at a white woman in Money, Mississippi, and sixteen years before the United States Supreme Court addressed Virginia's laws against interracial marriage in *Loving v. Virginia*.

A *New York Times* article in the early 1970s asked the intriguing question, "Why Does White America Love Sidney Poitier So?" Poitier was one of the early blacks to achieve Hollywood celebrity without clowning and shuffling—without overt compromising and accommodating. The same question could have been asked about Ray Robinson in 1950.

Sugar Ray reached a pinnacle of adulation most athletes only dream about. His star had faded by the time of the 1965 farewell evening and has continued to dim since his death two decades ago. Robinson only ranked 24th on the ESPN's *SportsCentury* top 50 list (Michael Jordan was number 1), a far cry from his extraordinary popularity in the 1940s and 1950s.

It's compelling to reflect on his life and his era in these unique sports times: War is raging in Iraq and Afghanistan, but Congress focuses on a celebrity sports scandal—steroid use; the NBA's Ron Artest atones for his bad behavior by hawking CDs on the *Today Show*; Ricky Williams, studying ancient Chinese medicine under the Northern California redwoods at Grass Valley's College of Ayurveda, walks away from millions to smoke dope; and Latrell Sprewell proclaims he can't feed his family on $7 million per year, but most of America misses his point. An alleged rape haunts Kobe Bryant, and Terrell Owens doesn't realize that a towel-dropping episode on a *Monday Night Football* broadcast, costarring an actress from *Desperate Housewives*, might not have been what the fans had tuned in to see (or maybe he does), and in the not too distant past there was the tragedy of O. J. Simpson.

Sugar Ray Robinson recognized the power of celebrity decades before other athletes even dreamed of taking their game beyond the field of play. Robinson certainly had his faults. But those faults foretold the shortcomings of today's athletes as well. His problems—with women, with money, with not knowing when to retire, with not always showing the world the personality it expected—all of these are ingredients of an increasingly coherent celebrity athlete formula.

Most of today's athletes, as well as modern fans, are totally unaware that Sugar Ray Robinson fought their battles, battled their demons, and enjoyed or endured much that was best and worst in modern sports superstardom half a century before anyone else took that exhilarating climb—or fatal plunge.

It is difficult for any athlete, no matter what their race, to achieve all that Robinson achieved—in one career. You have to recognize, too, that each celebrity is a product of his or her time. For that reason alone, no one could truly be Sugar Ray. That makes Robinson less a role model for today's youth than a potential spiritual mentor for our pro athletes.

Sugar Ray Robinson understood the commodification of celebrity—particularly the black performer in sports and entertainment—and made the system serve his needs. He displayed remarkable pride, power, and grace under every kind of pressure. Unlike many contemporary superstars, on occasion Robinson publicly showed a degree of social consciousness that was as profound as it was subtle.

"George Bush doesn't care about black people." In 2005, in the midst of the Hurricane Katrina aftermath, the performing artist Kanye West captured media attention with his impromptu statement in the midst of a network fundraising broadcast. This was one of the infrequent political statements by a celebrity, black or white, and they are even rarer from athletes. Why aren't there more individuals speaking out? John Carlos, nearly forty years after his Olympic protest, said it is a question of "brains and balls." "Look, it's rare that a man has the combination of both." And it takes both, Carlos maintained, to risk an athletic career to make a political statement. It is also rare that the combination of both exists and a platform presents itself to that unique person. Carlos and Smith on a victory stand, Kellen Winslow giving a Hall of Fame speech, Kanye West on a live television broadcast: It does not happen often and it is even rarer without strong political leadership on the issues of the day.

While writing this book, I sometimes mentioned my "Sugar Ray" project to people who nodded enthusiastically and then went on and on about their love for Sugar

Ray *Leonard*. They talked about how they enjoyed his commercials with his son, asking, "I wonder where little Ray is now?"

Wrong Sugar Ray.

This, of course, contrasted with those approaching eighty years old. "Man, he had that pink—excuse me I mean *flamingo* pink—Cadillac and those businesses," reminisces Arthur Lewis, a former Harlemite. "There was Sugar Ray's Café, a cleaner's, and a barbershop. A whole city block." The amazement comes through in Lewis's voice and eyes. Still holding court, Lewis pauses and looks at me with a smile, his mind's eye clearly seeing that Cadillac and the neon sign glowing *Sugar Ray's Café*. He leans back, says softly, reflectively, and sweetly, "Sugar Ray."

As great as Leonard was, in the words of Ralph Wiley, he could not be as great as Robinson unless he fought at least one hundred more times. Robinson entered the ring more than two hundred times; Leonard scarcely forty.

Sugar Ray Robinson was the consummate professional, entertainer, and businessperson. How do today's athletes measure up compared to Sugar Ray Robinson?

The modern athlete could take the best from Sugar Ray and not be doing too badly. Ray's life also provides clear warnings on what to look out for. You chisel a lot of this together. You take the fabulous Sugar Ray farewell and transition it into the George Foreman Grill, or Joe DiMaggio's Mr. Coffee, or David Robinson's or Andre Agassi's educational programs, Billie Jean King's Women's Sports

Foundation, or the positives of Jim Brown's Amer-I-Can. It's not easy to do. To be great in athletics might mean that God shorted you on some of the other tools needed to be the model celebrity athlete. Robinson did not have the empirical frame, the model upon which to build a successful celebrity life; but he was almost there. Today's athletes do have that advantage. They should study Ray and others. But most often they don't. They'll copy everything about Michael Jordan, including sticking his tongue out, but not enough will take the time to see what pieces of the business model he laid out that they could follow.

Those who have not stepped back to attempt to plot out their lives could do so much better. To a large extent, athletic success requires myopic vision. The fiftieth anniversary of the integration of Major League Baseball, celebrated in 1997, saddened me in this regard. It was ironic how many then current African American baseball players did not know who Jackie Robinson was. It became the embarrassing interview question of the year. It is similarly sad that the $80 million Muhammad Ali Center opens in Louisville, Kentucky, and only one athlete, Lennox Lewis, had made a financial contribution to the effort. Many athletes do much that is good, but these two events are not in that realm.

Celebrity is complex, but it is also about being who you are, you being something people—not just white people—like. The highest level of celebrity is achieved when you spend that currency. It's also achieving goals beyond the field of play—but again with a joyousness that is recognized as genuine.

There is no great evidence that Sugar Ray consciously led that postsegregation celebrity athlete transition. Maybe athletes today are accomplishing something unconsciously. Time will tell. One can dream of being a celebrity, but success is never guaranteed. Like Oscar, Emmy, or Grammy night, if there is a chance you'll win, you'd better have a speech prepared, and you'd better be you and genuine—or you'll miss the moment. Sugar Ray lived the moment.

Notes

Unless noted otherwise, all fight descriptions were developed by the author from viewing full versions where available and clips in some instances that were broadcast on network or cable, begged, borrowed or obtained via eBay (which was also the source of a funeral program and various photos) as well as media accounts from the event. Invaluable visual resources included: *Sugar Ray Robinson: Pound for Pound*, Big Fights Inc. (1978); ESPN's *SportsCentury, #24 Sugar Ray Robinson* (2000), and the HBO special, *Sugar Ray Robinson: Bright Lights, Dark Shadows of a Champion* (1998). A number of the fight films were provided by the Amateur Athletic Foundation Library in Los Angeles. Finally, numerous 1950s Robinson television appearances on the *Steve Allen Show* and *Omnibus* were viewed at the Library of Congress.

Preface: Why Sugar Ray?

xiv **"a Robinson who never deferred to whites":** Ralph Wiley, *Serenity: A Boxing Memoir 1989* (Henry Holt, 1989), p. 62.

xiv **"It was a different time":** Author's interview with Ralph Wiley.

xv **From inside a small wire cage:** Marilyn Chase, "Monkeys Are Willing to 'Pay' for a Glimpse of High-Status Apes," *Wall Street Journal*, February 11, 2005, sec. B, p. 3.

xvii   **"People are willing to pay money":** Chase, "Monkeys Are Willing to 'Pay.'"

xix   ***The Ring* magazine:** Bert Randolph Sugar, ed., *The Ring: 1981 Record Book and Boxing Encyclopedia* (New York: Atheneum, 1981).

xix   **Robinson owned thriving businesses:** Sugar Ray Robinson (with Dave Anderson), *Sugar Ray* (New York: DaCapo, 1970), p. 157; John Lardner, "Whiz Kid of Boxing and Business," *Negro Digest* (July 1951): p. 45.

xx   **"one of the most disgusting figures one is compelled to meet in his business":** Sam Lacy, "Sugar Ray Robinson: Big Fist, Little Conscience," *Afro-American*, May 28, 1960, p. 3. Jimmy Breslin held a similar opinion: "He is the same Sugar Ray Robinson— egotistical, hard to reach in conversation, but possessing rare color and individuality." Jimmy Breslin, "The Last Days of Sugar Ray," *Saturday Evening Post*, March 17, 1962, p. 106. From boxing promoters and the like much of this attitude was no doubt due to the difficult bargains he was likely to drive. He cancelled as many as fifty fights in his career, according to one count; see, for example, "Sugar Ray-Genius?" *Newsweek*, September 9, 1957, p. 98.

CHAPTER ONE: ADULATION

3   **a "cute chocolate baby":** ESPN's *SportsCentury* (2000).

3   **white faces turn jubilantly:** Portions of the retirement evening may be viewed in a number of documentaries. *Sugar Ray Robinson: Pound for Pound*, Big Fights Inc., 1978, provides an extensive contextual view. For a description of the evening's events, see Robinson, *Sugar Ray*, p. 362. There is also an extensive description and photos of the evening in "Sugar Ray's Farewell," *Amsterdam (NY) News*, December 18, 1965, p. 41. The pre-event press covered the story as well: "Sugar Ray to Say Farewell December 10," *Amsterdam (NY) News*, December 4, 1965, p. 37.

6   **"I'm sorry, but you'll have to pay me":** Robinson, *Sugar Ray*, p. 362.

6   **"finger-tip":** Breslin, "The Last Days of Sugar Ray," p. 106.

7   **black heavyweight champion Jack Johnson:** The best examina-
     tion of the impact of Jack Johnson is in Al-Tony Gilmore, *Bad
     Nigger! The National Impact of Jack Johnson* (Port Washington,
     NY: Kennikut Press, 1975).

8   **Emile Griffith killed Benny "Kid" Paret:** Joyce Carol Oates,
     On Boxing (Garden City, NY: Dolphin/Doubleday, 1987), p. 89.

10   **Nat King Cole:** For a full examination of his life see Leslie
     Gourse, *Unforgettable: The Life and Mystique of Nat King Cole*
     (New York: St. Martin's Press, 2000), p. 191.

13   **"What's worse—being a has-been or a never-was?":** Wiley,
     Serenity, p. 210. Sid Lockitch, Robinson's business manager dur-
     ing his retired Los Angeles years repeated a similar story to me.
     Author's interview with Sid Lockitch.

14   **Noticeably missing is . . . Jake La Motta:** Robinson, *Sugar Ray*,
     p. 363.

15   **"a tout a l'heure":** Robinson, *Sugar Ray*, p. 363.

18   **"I think we're supposed to leave":** Ibid., p. 364.

19   **big trophy reverentially on the hardwood floor:** Robinson, *Sugar
     Ray*, pp. 364–365. Author's interview with Dave Anderson.

19   **"I went through four million dollars":** Robinson, *Sugar Ray*,
     pp. 3–4 and 367; Breslin, "The Last Days of Sugar Ray," p. 106.

CHAPTER TWO: BEGINNINGS

21   **born on May 3, 1921:** Robinson, *Sugar Ray*, p. 8. Research did
     uncover a birth certificate from the Georgia State Board of
     Health, Bureau of Vital Statistics #46414. It shows Walker
     Smith's date of birth in Ailey, Georgia, as May 3, 1921. An earlier
     biography by Gene Schoor lists the birth date at May 3, 1920, and
     refers to his birthplace as Detroit's Paradise Valley, which is actu-
     ally a small entertainment subsection of Black Bottom. Gene
     Schoor, *Sugar Ray Robinson: World's Greatest Fighter—Pound for
     Pound* (New York: Greenberg, 1951), p. 1. Another biographer,
     Thomas Myler, goes with 1920 as well. See Thomas Myler, *Sugar
     Ray Robinson: The Inside Story* (Dublin, Ireland: Relym Publica-
     tions, 1996).

22   **in his mother's womb:** Robinson, *Sugar Ray*, p. 8.

22 **"They wrote back about how easy it was to get a job":** Ibid., p. 7.

22 **back to Georgia:** Ibid., p. 10.

23 **"a few drinks now and then":** Ibid., 9.

23 **Mama, who was a seamstress:** Schoor, *Sugar Ray Robinson*, p. 2.

23 **back to Detroit:** Robinson, *Sugar Ray*, p. 13.

23 **the tattered gym bag of Joe Louis Barrow:** The story is a bit apocryphal and is told over and over again. Schoor, *Sugar Ray Robinson*, p. 10; Robinson, *Sugar Ray*, p. 14. His mother told *Time* magazine the story of the relationship between the two boxers was "baloney." See "Businessman Boxer," *Time*, June 2, 1951, p. 58.

24 **Black Bottom:** Robinson, *Sugar Ray*, p. 7. That said, one source indicates the name was related to the dark soil. Peter Gavrilovich and Bill McGraw, eds., *The Detroit Almanac: 300 Years of Life in the Motor City* (Detroit: Detroit Free Press, 2000), p. 108.

26 **Dr. Vincent Nardiello:** Schoor, *Sugar Ray Robinson*, p. 24.

26 **Brewster Recreation Center:** Robinson, *Sugar Ray*, pp. 13–15. Schoor, *Sugar Ray Robinson*, pp. 8–11.

27 **"something wrong with his head":** Robinson, *Sugar Ray*, p. 15.

31 **taping his hands with Kotex tampons:** Sam Toperoff, *Sugar Ray Leonard and Other Noble Warriors* (New York: McGraw-Hill, 1987), p. 68.

32 **"I started flailing":** Robinson, *Sugar Ray*, p. 32.

32 **Benny Booksinger:** Ibid., p. 33.

32 **George Gainford:** Ibid., pp. 37–54. Schoor, *Sugar Ray Robinson*, pp. 21–29.

34 **an old Victrola:** Breslin, "The Last Days of Sugar Ray," p. 106. This story of the nickname "Sugar" has been retold in numerous ways as well, but it is always some version of the exchange noted in the text. Robinson, for example, tells the story in *Sugar Ray*, pp. 43–47, absent the Victrola.

35 **Robinson and Louis Valentine:** Ibid., pp. 69–70.

41 **"Referee Bernie Newman stepped between the fighters":** Joseph P. Nichols, "Golden Gloves Finals in Garden Ring Thrill Crowd of 17,032," *New York Times*, February 20, 1940, p. 29.

43 **Joe Louis was always *handled*:** Julie Salamon, "In This Corner, Joe Louis; in the Other, Forces of Evil," *New York Times*, June 22,

2000, sec. E, p. 9. Joe Louis (with Art and Edna Rust), *My Life* (New York: Harcourt, 1978). For a compelling story of the struggles and relationship of Joe Louis and Jesse Owens, see Donald McRae, *Heroes Without a Country: America's Betrayal of Joe Louis and Jesse Owens* (New York: Ecco, 2003).

43   **"Jack Johnson had failed to garner popular appeal":** See, generally, Gilmore, *The National Impact of Jack Johnson*.

43   **Jackie Robinson was enmeshed:** For a thorough understanding of the deal Robinson struck with Branch Rickey and the struggles he endured in doing so, see Jules Tygiel, *Baseball's Great Experiment: Jackie Robinson and His Legacy* (New York: Oxford University Press, 1997).

43   **"Champion of America":** William C. Rhoden, *Forty Million Dollar Slaves: The Rise, Fall, and Redemption of the Black Athlete* (New York: Crown, 2006), p. 38.

44   **Booker T. Washington began to wax negatively:** "Jack Johnson has harmed rather than helped," Gilmore, *The National Impact of Jack Johnson*, p. 5.

44   **Isaac Murphy:** Kenneth L. Shropshire, *In Black and White: Race and Sports in America* (New York: New York University Press, 1996), p. 27.

44   **Major Taylor:** For a contextual discussion of Taylor's life and his impact in cycling, see Rhoden, *Forty Million Dollar Slaves*, pp. 84–91.

45   **Before the institution of the black exclusionary rule:** Shropshire, *In Black and White*, p. 28.

47   **France was the prime destination for "colored troops":** See, generally, William A. Shack, *Harlem and Montmarte: A Paris Jazz Story Between the Great Wars* (Berkeley: University of California, 2001).

47   **Smith family moved to Hell's Kitchen:** Robinson, *Sugar Ray*, p. 21.

52   **Curt Horrmann:** Robinson, *Sugar Ray*, p. 71.

53   **"Private Robinson":** *The Ring*, September, 1943; Robinson, *Sugar Ray*, pp. 120–129; Schoor, *Sugar Ray Robinson*, pp. 51–54.

54   **he would not participate in the fixes:** Robinson, *Sugar Ray*, pp. 179–187.

55 **"'You'd *darken* the class'"**: W. C. Heinz, "The Greatest, Pound for Pound," in *Once They Heard the Cheers,* in Jeff Silverman, ed., *The Greatest Boxing Stories Ever Told* (Guilford, CT: Lyons Press, 2002), p. 275.

55 **"In this country"**: Heinz, "The Greatest, Pound for Pound," p. 275.

56 **that big nigger waiting for you:** For a thorough discussion of the role of Sonny Liston in society, see Nick Tosches, *The Devil and Sonny Liston* (Boston: Little, Brown, 2000).

CHAPTER THREE: HEROES

61 **Halloran General Hospital:** Schoor, *Sugar Ray Robinson*, p. 53. Robinson, *Sugar Ray,* pp. 120–129 (for the text of Robinson's personal account). Herb Boyd, *Pound for Pound: A Biography of Sugar Ray Robinson* (New York: Amistad, 2005), pp. 67–77.

62 **did not even recognize his wife:** Robinson, *Sugar Ray,* p. 128.

63 **"But why would a man say such a thing?":** Heinz, "The Greatest, Pound for Pound," p. 288.

63 **"conflicting versions" of events:** Ibid., p. 278.

63 **"You may be a good fighter":** Robinson, *Sugar Ray,* p. 130.

64 **unflattering column, written by Dan Parker:** Ibid., p. 129.

65 **"Save me, Joe Louis. Save me, Joe Louis. Save me, Joe Louis":** Oates, *On Boxing,* p. 62.

66 **Pat Tillman:** Richard Lacayo, "One for the Team," *Time,* May 3, 2004, p. 38.

69 **"Let's hope, *now* that sports are in perspective":** Rick Reilly, "It's A Whole New Ballgame," *Sports Illustrated,* October 1, 2001, p. 88.

70 **Usually, the press didn't dig deeply:** Author's interview with Bert Randolph Sugar.

71 **"Don't be like me":** Dave Anderson, "I'll Try to Make Up for Stuff," *New York Times,* July 12, 1995, sec. B, p. 9.

71 **"no longer see me as a role model":** Lois Romano, "Remorse from a Heavyweight; Morrison Grieves Over Lifestyle That Led to HIV," *Washington Post,* February 16, 1996, sec. A, p. 1.

71 **"He's a great role model":** Steve Wieberg, "Magic Offers Morrison Advice About HIV Situation," *USA Today,* February 16, 1996, sec. C, p. 3.

72   **"I am not a role model"**: "Wreaking Havoc—and Selling Sneaks," *New York Times*, June 2, 1993, sec. A, p. 18.

73   **"I'm not trying to get Cheerio commercials"**: Liz Robbins, "Artest's Next Battle Will Be to Revive Career," *New York Times*, July 17, 2005, p. 8.

74   **Jim Brown**: See generally, Jim Brown (with Steve Delsohn), *Out of Bounds* (New York: Zebra Books, 1989).

75   **O. J. Simpson was the first successful crossover**: Author's interview with Todd Boyd.

75   **withheld his support from Harvey Gantt**: Charles Pierce, Citizen Jordan, http://www.slate.com/id/2112224, January 13, 2005. Arguably the criticisms are unfair if for no other reason than because he is reported to have made monetary contributions to Gantt, http://www.newsmeat.com/sports_political_donations/Michael_Jordan.php indicating donations of $2,000 in the primary and general senatorial campaign. See also David Halberstam, *Playing for Keeps: Michael Jordan and the World He Made* (New York: Random House, 1999).

75   **Jordan explained on *60 Minutes***: http://www.cbsnews.com/stories/2005/10/19/60minutes/main955628.shtml.

77   **watch reruns of *Eyes on the Prize***: The best analysis of this changing generational civil rights perspective is in Todd Boyd, *The New H.N.I.C.: The Death of Civil Rights and the Reign of Hip Hop* (New York: New York University Press, 2004).

78   **His insistence on an integrated audience**: Robinson, *Sugar Ray*, pp. 120–124.

78   **The story of Kellen Winslow Jr.**: Author's interview with Kellen Winslow Sr. For background information, see Wayne Drehs, "A Racial Divide Between Father and Son," http://www.rlrassociates.net/clients/winslow–2.html.

80   **Sugar Ray was also no Ted Williams**: Rod Beaton, "Baseball Great Ted Williams Dies," *USA Today*, July 22, 2002, http://www.usatoday.com/sports/baseball/williams/ted-obit.htm. The article discusses Williams as a war hero who essentially gave up nearly five years of his baseball career while in the service (three years during World War II and almost two in the Korean conflict, where he flew thirty-nine combat missions).

81   **"I went where they sent me in the Army. A fellow of my color doesn't buck them":** "Ray Robinson Gets Officer's Backing," *New York Times*, May 9, 1954, p. 42.

82   **"We were over there, Joe Louis and I":** Heinz, "The Greatest, Pound for Pound," p. 288.

CHAPTER FOUR: STYLE

83   **"the black lights of unconsciousness":** Thomas Hauser, *The Black Lights: Inside the World of Professional Boxing* (New York: McGraw Hill, 1986), preface. Ali went on to say in this 1967 quote: "But I don't know nothing about that. I've had twenty-eight fights and twenty-eight wins. I ain't never been stopped."

83   **title vacated by Marty Servo:** James Goodrich, "Fighter Without a Fight," *Negro Digest*, June 1956, pp. 11–14, discusses the difficulty Robinson had in getting a title bout.

84   **the uncrowned champ:** Author's interview with Bert Randolph Sugar.

85   **Bell goes down. . . . Bell staggers back to his feet:** James P. Dawson, "Robinson Beats Bell on Points for World Welterweight Title Before 15,670," *New York Times*, December 21, 1946, p. 22.

86   **The idea of a pink Caddy:** H. Boyd, *Pound for Pound*, p. 101.

86   **big maroon Packard:** Ibid., p. 38. Robinson may have been aware of the stylings of Jack Johnson as well: "Good clothes and plenty of them, enough diamonds to illuminate his shirt front to make him a conspicuous figure when he promenades the streets . . . seldom does a day pass but what he will appear on the streets three or four times in changed attire from head to foot." Gilmore, *The National Impact of Jack Johnson*, p. 17.

87   **"When my car arrived":** Robinson, *Sugar Ray*, p. 155.

87   **"Hope Diamond":** Ibid.

88   **"Oh—she really loved that pink Cadillac!":** Author's interview with François Balsan.

88   **"When you're a kid":** Jake La Motta, *Raging Bull* (New York: Bantam Books, 1980), p. 3. As his career progressed he, too, got a Cadillac, a convertible as well, p. 127.

88   **"Rookie year, I purchased a Cadillac convertible":** Jim Brown, *Out of Bounds*, p. 125.

88   **headquarters of the entire Robinson empire:** Robinson, *Sugar Ray*, p. 157. The establishments are referred to by various names in articles and other books, but those listed here appear to be the most consistent.

90   ***The White Negro:*** Norman Mailer, "The White Negro," in Nicolaus Mills, ed., *Legacy of Dissent: Forty Years of Writing from Dissent Magazine* (New York: Simon & Schuster, 1994), pp. 53–173.

90   **the embrace of black culture:** See also Lewis MacAdams, *Birth of the Cool: Beat Bebop and the American Avant Garde* (New York: The Free Press, 2001). For a discussion of cool cat black men, see Richard Majors and Janet Mancini Billson, *Cool Pose: The Dilemmas of Black Manhood in America* (New York: Lexington Books, 1992); and regarding African Americans and style generally, see Shane White and Graham White, *Stylin': African American Expressive Culture from Its Beginnings to the Zoot Suit* (Ithaca, NY: Cornell University Press, 1998).

92   **Davis told his biographer, Quincy Troupe:** Miles Davis (with Quincy Troupe), *Miles: The Autobiography* (New York: Simon & Schuster, 1989), p. 174.

93   **Robinson fought Rocky Graziano:** Joseph C. Nichols, "Robinson Choice to Keep the Title Against Graziano Tonight," *New York Times*, April 16, 1952, p. 37.

98   **Graziano also carried . . . a dishonorable discharge:** Heinz, "The Greatest, Pound for Pound," p. 277.

99   **"The NFL powers look exceptionally stupid and petty":** *"Pardon the Interruption,"* ESPN, May 9, 2005.

101   **"Every player should have a feel of how they market their own selves":** Shira Springer, "Dress Code Wears Thin with Pierce," *Boston Globe*, October 20, 2005, sec. D, p. 1.

102   **NBA dress code:** Memo from David Stern to NBA Players: "NBA Player Dress Code," October 17, 2005.

102   **"The whole thing is fake":** Janie McCauley, "Richardson Against NBA's New Dress Code," AP, October 20, 2005, BC cycle (Nexis).

103   **Robinson home was featured in *Ebony* magazine:** "'Sugar Ray' Robinson's Dream House," *Ebony*, June 1953, p. 41.

103   **"the kind of home I've wanted all of my life":** Ibid.

104   **Chamberlain's house:** Gary M. Pomerantz, *Wilt, 1962* (New York: Crown, 2005), pp. 2–3.

Chapter Five: Rivalries

107 **On Valentine's Day:** James P. Dawson, "Robinson Knocks Out La Motta in 13th," *New York Times*, February 15, 1951, p. 43.

110 **Years later, at a fifty-something birthday party:** Shelden Schiffman, *Sugar Ray Robinson: Beyond the Boxer* (Nashville, TN: Express Media, 2004), p. 78.

112 **Larry Holmes-Randall "Tex" Cobb bloodbath:** Larry Holmes (with Phil Berger), *Larry Holmes Against the Odds* (New York: St. Martin's Press, 1998), pp. 214–216.

114 **"You never put me down, Ray!":** From the film *Raging Bull* (1980). In his autobiography, Ray writes that he knew what La Motta was thinking: "*You didn't put me on the deck, Robinson. You got my title, but you didn't put me on the deck.*" Robinson, *Sugar Ray*, p. 185.

115 **"I fought Sugar Ray six times in all":** La Motta, *Raging Bull*, p. 124.

115 **"He was a nemesis to me":** Ibid.

115 **"I mean he wasn't exactly a pansy":** Ibid., p. 101.

116 **Tex Rickard, sought permission:** Gilmore, *The National Impact of Jack Johnson*, p. 33.

117 **President Reagan had a phone line installed:** Holmes, *Larry Holmes Against the Odds*, p. 207.

120 **Martina-Chrissie:** For a discussion of one of the greatest rivalries, see Johnette Howard, *The Rivals: Chris Evert vs. Martina Navratilova: Their Epic Duels and Extraordinary Friendship* (New York: Broadway Books, 2005).

121 **"There were no workouts":** Gordon Parks, *Voices in the Mirror* (New York: Harlem Moon/Broadway Books, 2005), p. 193.

124 **He even journeyed from Southampton, England:** "Turpin Is En Route for Robinson Bout," *New York Times*, August 15, 1951, p. 44.

127 **"That referee should not have stopped the bout":** "Did Turpin Make Sugar Ray Quit Boxing," *Our World*, November 1953, p. 71–74.

127 **They stormed the doors at the State Lake Theatre:** Jack Gould, "Theatres Packed, Fan Stampede at Video Showings of Title Fight," *New York Times*, September 13, 1951, p. 41.

127   **With a gate of $768,000:** "New York," *New York Times*, September 16, 1951, sec. E, p. 2.

131   **"Rocky Marciano couldn't hold my jock strap":** Holmes, *Larry Holmes Against the Odds*, p. 236. In this postfight interview, Holmes tried to clean it up and complimented Marciano, but as Holmes noted in his autobiography: "The insult is halfway around the world before the apology gets its boots on," p. 237.

CHAPTER SIX: OVERREACHING

135   **He was quite a terrible singer:** Sugar Ray Robinson, *Bright Lights, Dark Shadows of a Champion*, HBO, 1998.

135   **"I am here to meet with Mr. Weintraub":** *Sugar Ray Robinson: Pound for Pound*, Big Fights Inc., 1978.

136   **possibility that a bout with Floyd Patterson:** "Ray Robinson Listens to $Million Offer," *Journal and Guide*, June 14, 1958, p. 14, and Joe Bostic, "Even for a Million Robinson-Patterson Doesn't Figure," *New York Age*, June 14, 1958, p. 32. Additionally, the historian Bert Sugar noted simply: "It was not going to happen." Not for any other reason than, "Robinson was simply too difficult to deal with." Author's interview with Randolph Bert Sugar.

136   **Archie Moore:** For similar reasons, Bert Sugar says this was not about to happen either and that Moore became thoroughly disgusted with Robinson's overbearing, demanding negotiations. See, for example, "Archie, Sugar Trade Barbs," *Chicago Defender*, May 30, 1959, p. 23, and "Moore-Robby Head for Ring Showdown In Million $ Bout," *Journal and Guide*, March 3, 1959, p. 24.

137   **Stanley Ketchel, to fight Jack Johnson:** Geoffrey C. Ward, *Unforgivable Blackness: The Rise and Fall of Jack Johnson* (New York: Alfred A. Knopf, 2004), pp. 158–163.

137   **he was a reluctant celebrity:** See Floyd Patterson, *Victory Over Myself* (New York: Alfred A. Knopf, 1963).

138   **"you don't laugh at a million dollars":** "Ray Robinson Listens to $Million Offer," *Journal and Guide*, June 14, 1958, p. 14.

138   **the best have always understood:** One of the first was the Galloping Ghost, Harold "Red" Grange, who may be pointed to as

the first who understood the entertainment crossover in the 1920s. See John M. Carroll, *Red Grange and the Rise of Modern Football* (Champaign: University of Illinois Press, 1999).

139 **"The people wanted to see me fight"**: *Sugar Ray Robinson: Pound for Pound*, Big Fights Inc., 1978.

140 **"Turkish bath"**: H. Boyd, *Pound for Pound*, p. 140.

142 **"The referee grew more hair"**: Schiffman, *Sugar Ray Robinson*, p. 87.

143 **Maxim shrugs it off**: Arthur Dailey, "Sports of the Times: A Triumph for Mediocrity," June 27, 1952, p. 27.

143 **"Robinson, a smart fighter, didn't fight a smart fight"**: Arthur Dailey, "Sports of the Times: A Triumph for Mediocrity," June 27, 1952, p. 27.

143 **"I do not feel I can any longer"**: Joseph C. Nichols, "Robinson Retires From Ring, Gives Up Middleweight Title," *New York Times*, December 19, 1952, p. 41. Regarding retiring following this bout, Robinson said: "I could see the opening in a flash and, in the same twinkle, handle the situation. Now the co-ordination isn't there any more. No one knows that better than I do." Joseph C. Nichols, "Decision Revealed by Greene of N.B.A.," *New York Times*, December 19, 1952, p. 41.

144 **Intravenous fluids**: H. Boyd, *Pound for Pound*, p. 143.

144 **"Did I have air conditioning in my corner?"**: Edward Wong, "Joey Maxim Dies at 79; Outlasted Sugar Ray Robinson," *New York Times*, June 5, 2001, sec. B, p. 10.

145 **Class AA Birmingham Barons**: http://www.nba.com/playerfile/ michael_jordan/bio.html.

146 **"remove scar tissue from beneath the eyes"**: "Sugar Ray's New Face," *Our World*, January 1953, pp. 40–43.

146 **Johnson . . . went on to bullfighting**: Gilmore, *The National Impact of Jack Johnson*, p. 152.

147 **NBA stars . . . as rappers**: Soren Baker, "Top Athletes Own a Piece of the Rap," *New York Times*, July 14, 1997, sec. D, p. 9; and Annie Hoffman, "Jock Jams: Sports Stars Hitting High Notes in Music Industry." Included in this work about athletes transitioning to entertainment is the wrestler turned actor, "The Rock," Dwayne Johnson. See *The Rock* (with Joe Layden), *The Rock Says* (New York: Regan Books, 2000).

148   **Robinson earned . . . $10,000 per week:** "A Perfectionist Retires," *Time*, December 29, 1952, p. 31.

148   **"second-rate song and dance man":** "The Final Bell," *Time*, January 31, 1955, p. 42.

149   **"I know one thing":** Ibid.

149   **George Gainford and Harry Wiley . . . quit:** H. Boyd, *Pound for Pound*, p. 160.

150   **"This is something I never thought could possibly happen":** Mark Bresnahan, "Lakers Turn to Hire Power," *Los Angeles Times*, June 15, 2005, sec. A, p. 1.

CHAPTER SEVEN: ENTOURAGE

155   **"We just couldn't leave anybody":** "Sugar in Paris," *Time*, January 1, 1951, p. 36.

157   **Duke Ellington . . . gushed, "You can go anywhere":** Luke Miner, *Paris Jazz* (New York: The Little Bookroom, 2005), p. 6. See also Tyler Stovall, *Paris Noir* (New York: Houghton Mifflin, 1996).

158   **like so many blacks who had visited Paris before him:** Schoor, *Sugar Ray Robinson*, p. 100.

159   **determined to obtain permission to visit the notorious facility:** H. Boyd, *Pound for Pound*, p. 135.

159   **"They were deserting the sinking ship.":** Ibid., p. 160.

160   **Allen Iverson:** For the deepest understanding of the uniquely supportive background that forms the basis of Iverson's loyalty to his family and friends see Larry Platt, *Only the Strong Survive: The Odyssey of Allen Iverson* (New York: Regan Books, 2002).

162   **"See, you've got to understand Black people":** Larry Platt, "Magic Johnson Builds an Empire," *The New York Times*, December 10, 2000, Sec. 6, p. 119.

164   **Damon Runyon Cancer Fund:** Robinson, *Sugar Ray*, p. 162 promising to donate his entire $25,000 purse from a fight with Robert Villemain, less one dollar, to the Damon Runyon Cancer Fund in the memory of one-time stable mate and opponent Spider Valentine who had died of cancer. See also, "'Hardest Dollar,' Champion Admits," *New York Times*, March 15, 1952, p. 16. Discussing Robinson also giving all but one dollar of his purse for a fight with Carl "Bobo" Olson.

165 **$12,500, to the mother of Jimmy Doyle:** Robinson, *Sugar Ray*, p. 144.

165 **Sugar Ray Robinson Youth Foundation:** Author's interview with Sid Lockitch. See "Whatever Happened to Sugar Ray Robinson?" *Ebony*, June 1978, p. 131.

CHAPTER EIGHT: PROBLEMS

169 **"Mr. and Mrs. Sugar Ray Robinson!":** H. Boyd, *Pound for Pound*, p. 166.

169 **"I was taught to obey the Ten Commandments":** Robinson, *Sugar Ray*, p. 6.

170 **"Paternity Ward":** Grant Wahl, Jon Wertheim, Lester Munson, Don Yeager, "Paternity Ward," *Sports Illustrated*, May 4, 1998, p. 62.

171 **Sugar Ray's first child:** Robinson, *Sugar Ray*, p. 59.

171 **Eventually, the marriage was annulled:** H. Boyd, *Pound for Pound*, p. 34.

171 **One writer determined that it was a divorce:** Schoor, *Sugar Ray Robinson*, p. 78.

172 **"The man was incredible":** H. Boyd, *Pound for Pound*, p. 198.

172 **Robinson's dalliances were heartbreaking:** H. Boyd, *Pound for Pound*, p. 166.

173 **Mike Tyson . . . rape conviction in 1992:** See Peter Heller, *Bad Intentions: The Mike Tyson Story* (New York: DaCapo, 1995).

173 **NBA star Kobe Bryant:** "Kobe admits adultery, denies raping woman," July 18, 2003, Kevin Modesti Inland Valley Daily Bulletin.com, http://u.sbsun.com/Stories/0,1413,203%257E28728%257E1520830,00.html.

174 **81-point total:** John Eligon, "An 81 Point Argument for Bryant Being the Best," *New York Times*, January 24, 2006, sec. D, p. 5.

175 **Randy Moss . . . told Bryant Gumbel:** HBO *Heal Sports with Bryant Gumbel*, Episode 101, August 23, 2005; AP, "Raiders' Moss Admits Using Marijuana," *New York Times*, August 19, 2005, sec. D, p. 4.

177 **"It was alcohol consumption by both parents":** Robinson, *Sugar Ray*, pp. 9–10.

177   **Vitamin B-12:** Ibid., 285.

178   **"a glass of beef blood?":** Ferdie Pacheco (with Jim Moskovitz),
       The 12 Greatest Rounds of Boxing: The Untold Stories (Toronto:
       Sports Classic Books, 2003), p. 67. For a slightly different ver-
       sion of the same tale, see Robinson, *Sugar Ray*, p. 183.

179   **Vincent Nardiello, who reportedly stopped speaking to Ray:**
       Breslin, "The Last Days of Sugar Ray," p. 106.

180   **Terrell Owens:** Paul Vigna, "Hard One to Top," *Philadelphia
       Daily News*, September 28, 2006, http://www.philly.com/mld/
       dailynews/sports/15626574.htm.

182   **"'What's-in-it-for-me?'":** "Businessman Boxer," *Time*, June 25,
       1951, p. 64. There were accusations throughout his career that
       he would win and lose titles because he wanted to get paid the
       greater sums for rematches, see, for example, Lee D. Jenkins,
       "Sugar Reopens Lend-Lease Title Dealings," *Chicago Defender*,
       February 6, 1960, p. 23, "It's a foul question that indicates that
       there is some thought that Sugar's pet occupation is losing titles
       large or small, just so he can come back under more lucrative
       conditions and win 'em back."

183   ***Requiem for a Heavyweight:*** The 1962 film based on a 1956
       Rod Sterling teleplay focusing on the sad life of a washed-up,
       broke, punch-drunk boxer.

184   **Louis's heart muscles were damaged:** See his Michigan wrestling
       license at: http://www.michigan.gov/images/hal_mhc_sa_joelouis
       _card_50957_7.jpg.

184   **"I was threatened with foreclosures":** H. Boyd, *Pound for Pound*,
       p. 156. Breslin, "The Last Days of Sugar Ray," pp. 108–109. See
       also, A. S. "Doc" Young, "What Happened to Sugar Ray's
       Money?" *Jet*, February 19, 1955, 52–55. He denied being in trou-
       ble even as properties were lost. See, Evelyn Cunningham,
       "'Broke?' I'm Spread Out Too Thin'-Sugar Ray," *Courier*, March
       17, 1962, p. 7, and "Sugar Ray's Property to Be Auctioned," *Am-
       sterdam (NY) News*, March 10, 1962. See also Lester Bromberg,
       "What Happened to Joe Louis Won't Happen to Me!" *National
       Police Gazette*, July 1952, p. 16.

184   **$250,000 missing:** Breslin, "The Last Days of Sugar Ray,"
       p. 108.

185   **Mark McGwire . . . unsatisfactory turn as witness:** Sean Gregory, "Hearings Leave a Legend Stained, a Commissioner Under Fire and a Game Still Under Suspicion," *Time*, March 28, 2006.

CHAPTER NINE: DEATH

189   **He'd hold court at tables in Matteo's:** Schiffman does an insightful and intimate job of describing some of the evenings they had in those later years. Schiffman, *Sugar Ray Robinson*, p. 30.

190   **Millie became very protective of her husband:** Elmer Smith, a *Philadelphia Daily News* columnist, poignantly told me that Millie's role in Ray's life was a version of the role that Muhammad Ali's wife, Lonnie, plays: Author's interview with Elmer Smith. See also *Sugar Ray Robinson: Bright Lights, Dark Shadows of a Champion*, HBO, 1998.

190   **Jimmy Doyle's 1947 death:** Robinson, *Sugar Ray*, p. 140.

191   **"It's my business to get him in trouble":** Robinson, *Sugar Ray*, p. 143. Also see "Robinson Cleared in Death of Doyle," *New York Times*, June 27, 1947, p. 24.

191   **"Oh my God, look at that man":** Breslin, "The Last Days of Sugar Ray," p. 106.

191   **"I could see the shot coming":** Pacheco, *The 12 Greatest Rounds of Boxing*, p. 73.

191   **Young Joe Walcott:** Larry L. King, "Sugar: Down but Not Quite Out," *Sports Illustrated*, September 6, 1965, p. 160.

192   **"Ray, you're packing it in":** Pete Hamill, in HBO's *Sugar Ray Robinson: The Bright Lights*, is one of many recollecting this moment.

201   **"One thing. Fullmer":** "Grace Under Pressure," *Newsweek*, January 14, 1957, p. 54.

202   **"Aw, what would be the point?":** Martin Kane, "The Bitter End for Sugar Ray," *Sports Illustrated*, November 22, 1965, p. 89.

202   **on the set of the *Dirty Dozen*:** Brown, *Out of Bounds*, p. 173. In the perfect contrast in retirement to Robinson, as Brown phrased it, "I knew when you went from [All-Pro linebacker] Sam Huff to Raquel Welch, it wasn't exactly bad shit" (p. 174).

203   **showing how Alzheimer's hit Robinson:** Schiffman, *Sugar Ray Robinson*, pp. 80–81.

205   **"After that night ... anything can happen":** Wiley, *Serenity*, p. 65.

206   **the cause of death:** Dave Anderson, "Sugar Ray Robinson, 'Boxing's Best,' Is Dead," *New York Times*, April 13, 1989, sec. A, p. 1.

206   **"Some of us, we worry about":** Seth Mydans, "Boxing's 'Rhapsody in Black' Mourned," *New York Times*, April 20, 1989, sec. D, p. 23.

206   **"world had a way of standing still":** AP, "The Famous Pay Homage to Sugar Ray's Brilliance," *Chicago Tribune*, April 20, 1989, sec. C, p. 6.

206   **"Jesse Owens, Joe Louis":** Ibid.

207   **"Champions win events":** Ibid.

208   **"Eat your heart out, Don King!":** Michael Connelly, "Throng Joins In Tribute to Sugar Ray Robinson; Boxing Great Called Hero In and Out of Ring," *Los Angeles Times*, April 20, 1989, part 2, p. 1.

EPILOGUE: ON BEING SUGAR RAY

213   **"I wanted to be like Willie Mays":** Pat Jordan, "The Outcast," *New Yorker*, July 9, 2001, p. 42.

213   **"kissed the wife of the President of France":** "Sugar Ray Gives Mme. Auriol Kiss," *New York Times*, May 17, 1951, p. 20.

214   **negative commentary came from Edna Mae:** "Sugar Ray Conquers Paris, Loses Title," *Ebony*, September 1951, p. 91.

214   *Loving v. Virginia:* 388 U.S. 1; 87 S. Ct. 1817; 18 L. Ed. 2d 1010; 1967 U.S. LEXIS 1082.

215   **"Why Does White America":** "Why Does White America Love Sidney Poitier So?" Clifford Mason, *New York Times*, September 10, 1967, sec. 2, p. 1. For more on Poitier, see Sidney Poitier, *The Measure of a Man: A Spiritual Autobiography* (New York: HarperCollins, 2000). For a solid academic essay on Robinson's positioning in popular culture see, David A. Nathan, "Sugar Ray Robinson, the Sweet Science and the Politics of Meaning" *Journal of Sports History* 26, no. 1 (Spring 1999): pp. 163–174.

215   **ESPN's *SportsCentury* top 50 list:** http://espn.go.com/ sportscentury/athletes.html.z

217   **"brains and balls":** Author's interview with John Carlos.

218   **Arthur Lewis, a former Harlemite:** Author's interview with
       Arthur Lewis.

218   **in the words of Ralph Wiley:** Wiley, *Serenity*, p. 210.

219   **Muhammad Ali Center:** William C. Rhoden, "Ali Center Re-
       flects the Evolution of a Champion," *New York Times*, November
       21, 2005, sec. D, p. 7.

INDEX